New York Yankees 2019

A Baseball Companion

Edited by Patrick Dubuque, Aaron Gleeman and Bret Sayre

Baseball Prospectus

Craig Brown and Dave Pease, Consultant Editors
Rob McQuown and Harry Pavlidis, Statistics Editors

Copyright © 2019 by DIY Baseball, LLC.
All rights reserved

This book or any part thereof may not be reproduced or transmitted in any form or by any means, electronic or mechanical, including photocopying, recording, or by any information storage and retrieval system, without permission in writing from the publisher.

Limit of Liability/Disclaimer of Warranty: While the publisher and the author have used their best efforts in preparing this book, they make no representations or warranties with respect to the accuracy or completeness of the contents of this book and specifically disclaim any implied warranties of merchantability or fitness for a particular purpose. No warranty may be created or extended by sales representatives or written sales materials. The advice and strategies contained herein may not be suitable for your situation. You should consult with a professional where appropriate. Neither the publisher nor the author shall be liable for any loss of profit or any other commercial damages, including but not limited to special, incidental, consequential, or other damages.

Library of Congress Cataloging-in-Publication Data:
paperback
ISBN-13: 978-1-949332-18-6

Project Credits
Cover Design: Kathleen Dyson
Interior Design and Production: Jeff Pease, Dave Pease
Layout: Jeff Pease, Dave Pease

Baseball icon courtesy of Uberux, from https://www.shareicon.net/author/uberux

Ballpark diagram courtesy of Lou Spirito/THIRTY81 Project, https://thirty81project.com/

Manufactured in the United States of America
10 9 8 7 6 5 4 3 2 1

Table of Contents

Foreword v
    Rob Mains

Statistical Introduction vii

Part 1: Team Analysis

Table for Two: Previewing the 2019 New York Yankees 3
    Derek Albin and E.J. Fagan

Performance Graphs 7

2018 Team Performance 8

2019 Team Projections 9

Team Personnel 10

Yankee Stadium Stats 11

Yankees Team Analysis 13

Part 2: Player Analysis

Yankees Player Analysis 18

Yankees Prospects 95

Part 3: Featured Articles

The Hole in The Shift is Fixing Itself 109
    Russell Carleton

The State of the Quality Start 113
    Rob Mains

Heads-Up Hacking—The First Pitch 119
    Matthew Trueblood

A Hymn for the Index Stat 125
    Patrick Dubuque

Index of Names 129

Foreword

Rob Mains

Welcome to this companion of the 2019 New York Yankees. We at Baseball Prospectus are excited to provide this analysis of the Yankees.

Our website, Baseball Prospectus, is a leader in delivering high-quality commentary and data to baseball fans everywhere. To some, those words—commentary and data—appear mutually exclusive. There are people out there who believe that traditional analysis and advanced analytics must run on different paths. But the simplistic narrative of stats vs. traditionalists just isn't true. Every team's analytics department interacts with scouting, development, and major league operations with a common goal: Delivering a championship. New technologies, like radar tracking of pitch speeds and movement, enable talent evaluators to focus on qualitative aspects of pitching like mechanics and pitch sequencing. In-game strategies like infield shifts, based on batters' hit tendencies, help turn balls in play into outs. Hitters use information to adjust their swings to maximize run production.

All these numbers can seem, at best, intimidating, and at worst, counterproductive to the casual fan. Even as technology and analysis have embedded themselves deeply into the way teams run, it can often feel like statistics create a displacement between the viewer and the sport, breaking them out of the action. And yet every fan incorporates the numbers to some degree; stats like batting average and earned run average, so fundamental to how we talk about performance, are actually complicated formulas. They don't bother people because those formulas have become second nature, as easy to translate as the action on the field.

Along the way, new statistics have entered baseball's lexicon. You'll see some of them, like on-base percentage (which measures a batter's ability to get on base via walk, hit batter, or hit), OPS (on-base plus slugging), and average exit velocity (the speed of balls off a hitter's bat) on broadcasts. Others, like DRC+, might well be new to you. Some of them have been well-defined to the public, others haven't. That lack of context has created ambiguity. Fans know that a ball hit 100 mph is scorched, but does that mean extra bases? (Not if it's hit on the ground or high in the air it doesn't.)

For those who are amenable to them, the new statistics can increase the enjoyment and understanding of the game. They can help fans identify when a pitcher is tiring, when a stolen base or a bunt attempt makes sense (and, more often, when it doesn't), or how a team's lineup might be constructed. Websites like Baseball Prospectus add to that understanding by weaving metrics into the narrative of the game. That's the goal of this publication: to take some of the newer, more complicated statistics and make them as intuitive as the ones on the back of old baseball cards.

But you don't need to love analytics to love baseball. The fans at BP who worked together to write this guide are captivated first and foremost by the game itself. We're drawn to Aaron Judge's power, Francisco Lindor's glove, Billy Hamilton's speed and Patrick Corbin's slider and don't need numbers to tell us why they're so mesmerizing. The underlying statistics provide depth to the game that we all love.

We hope you'll find that this guide helps you better understand the Yankees. Our analysts have studied the team's major league personnel and its minor league affiliates to identify their strengths and weaknesses, both the obvious ones and those that only a careful dissection of players' performances—yes, including the data—can reveal. You don't need us to tell you who was good and who wasn't in 2018, but our models and writers can help you project how each player is going to perform this year and beyond, and appreciate the greatness of each new game as it unfolds. As in the sport itself, the human and analytic components combine to generate a deeper overall understanding.

Think back to the first time you saw a baseball game on a high-definition TV. You'd grown familiar with how the game looked and felt on a picture tube. But new TV allowed you to see details that you'd never seen before. That's how advanced statistics work. The game itself is why you're here and why you're buying this. (And, for that matter, why we wrote it.) The statistical measures provide the sharper focus, the detail, the depth of knowledge that you didn't have before, generating an overall superior picture. Enjoy the view.

—*Rob Mains is an author of Baseball Prospectus.*

Statistical Introduction

Sports are, fundamentally, a blend of athletic endeavor and storytelling. Baseball, like any other sport, tells its stories in so many ways: in the arc of a game from the stands or a season from the box scores, in photos, or even in numbers. At Baseball Prospectus, we understand that statistics don't replace observation or any of baseball's stories, but complement everything else that makes the game so much fun.

What stats help us with is with patterns and precision, variance and value. This book can help you learn things you may not see from watching a game or hundred, whether it's the path of a career over time or the breadth of the entire MLB. We'd also never ask you to choose between our numbers and the experience of viewing a game from the cheap seats or the comfort of your home; our publication combines running the numbers with observations and wisdom from some of the brightest minds we can find. But if you *do* want to learn more about the numbers beyond what's on the backs of player jerseys, let us help explain.

Offense

At the end of this past year, we've revised our methodology for determining batting value. Long-time readers of Baseball Prospectus will notice that we've retired True Average in favor of a new metric: Deserved Runs Created Plus (DRC+). Developed by Jonathan Judge and our stats team, this statistic measures everything a player does at the plate–reaching base, hitting for power, making outs, and moving runners over–and puts it on a scale where 100 equals league-average performance. A DRC+ of 150 is terrific, a DRC+ of 100 is average, and a DRC+ of 75 means you better be an excellent defender.

DRC+ also does a better job than any of our previous metrics in taking contextual factors into account. The model adjusts for how the park affects performance, but also for things like the talent of the opposing pitcher, value of different types of batted-ball events, league, temperature, and other factors. It's able to describe a player's expected offensive contribution than any other statistic we've found over the years, and also does a better job of predicting future performance as well.

The other aspect of run-scoring is baserunning, which we quantify using Baserunning Runs. BRR not only records the value of stolen bases (or getting caught in the act), but also accounts for a runner's ability to go first to third on a single or advance on a fly ball.

Defense

Where offensive value is *relatively* easy to identify and understand, defensive value is ... not. Over the past dozen years, the sabermetric community has focused mostly on stats based on zone data: a real-live human person records the type of batted ball and estimated landing location, and models are created that give expected outs. From there, you can compare fielders' actual outs to those expected ones. Simple, right?

Unfortunately, zone data has two major issues. First, zone data is recorded by commercial data providers who keep the raw data private unless you pay for it. (All the statistics we build in this book and on our website use public data as inputs.) That hurts our ability to test assumptions or duplicate results. Second, over the years it has become apparent that there's quite a bit of "noise" in zone-based fielding analysis. Sometimes the conclusions drawn from zone data don't hold up to scrutiny, and sometimes the different data provided by different providers don't look anything alike, giving wildly different results. Sometimes the hard-working professional stringers or scorers might unknowingly inflict unconscious bias into the mix: for example good fielders will often be credited with more expected outs despite the data, and ballparks with high press boxes tend to score more line drives than ones with a lower press box.

Enter our Fielding Runs Above Average (FRAA). For most positions, FRAA is built from play-by-play data, which allows us to avoid the subjectivity found in many other fielding metrics. The idea is this: count how many fielding plays are made by a given player and compare that to expected plays for an average fielder at their position (based on pitcher ground-ball tendencies and batter handedness). Then we adjust for park and base-out situations.

When it comes to catchers, our methodology is a little different thanks to the laundry list of responsibilities they're tasked with beyond just, well, catching and throwing the ball. By now you've probably heard about "framing" or the art of making umpires more likely to call balls outside the strike zone for strikes. To put this into one tidy number, we incorporate pitch tracking data (for the years it exists) and adjust for important factors like pitcher, umpire, batter, and home-field advantage using a mixed-model approach. This grants us a number for how many strikes the catcher is personally adding to (or subtracting from) his pitchers' performance ... which we then convert to runs added or lost using linear weights.

Framing is one of the biggest parts of determining catcher value, but we also take into account blocking balls from going past, whether a scorer deems it a passed ball or a wild pitch. We use a similar approach–one that really benefits from the pitch tracking data that tells us what ends up in the dirt and what doesn't. We also include a catcher's ability to prevent stolen bases and how well they field balls in play, and *finally* we come up with our FRAA for catchers.

Pitching

Both pitching and fielding make up the half of baseball that isn't run scoring: run prevention. Separating pitching from fielding is a tough task, and most recent pitching analysis has branched off from Voros McCracken's famous (and controversial) statement, "There is little if any difference among major-league pitchers in their ability to prevent hits on balls hit in the field of play." The research of the analytic community has validated this to some extent, and there are a host of "defense-independent" pitching measures that have been developed to try and extricate the effect of the defense behind a hurler from the pitcher's work.

Our solution to this quandry is Deserved Run Average (DRA), our core pitching metric. DRA looks like earned run average (ERA), the tried-and-true pitching stat you've seen on every baseball broadcast or box score from the past century, but it's very different. To start, DRA takes an event-by-event look at what the pitchers does, and adjusts the value of that event based on different environmental factors like park, batter, catcher, umpire, base-out situation, run differential, inning, defense, home field advantage, pitcher role, and temperature. That mixed model gives us a pitcher's expected contribution, similar to what we do for our DRC+ model for hitters and FRAA model for catchers. (Oh, and we also consider the pitcher's effect on basestealing and on balls getting past the catcher.)

It's important to note that DRA is set to the scale of runs allowed per nine innings (RA9) instead of ERA, which makes DRA's scale slightly higher than ERA's. The reason for this is because ERA tends to overrate three types of pitchers:

1. Pitchers who play in parks where scorers hand out more errors. Official scorers differ significantly in the frequency at which they assign errors to fielders.
2. Ground-ball pitchers, because a substantial proportion of errors occur on grounders.
3. Pitchers who aren't very good. Better pitchers often allow fewer unearned runs than bad pitchers, because good pitchers tend to find ways to get out of jams.

Since the last time you picked up an edition of this book, we've also made a few minor changes to DRA to make it better. Recent research into "tunneling"–the act of throwing consecutive pitches that appear similar from a batter's point of view until after the swing decision point–data has given us a new contextual factor to account for in DRA: plate distance. This refers to the distance between successive pitches as they approach the plate, and while it has a smaller effect than factors like velocity or whiff rate, it still can help explain pitcher strikeout rate in our model.

New Pitching Metrics for 2019

We're including a few "new" pitching metrics for 2019's suite of Baseball Prospectus publications, but you may be familiar with them if you've spent time scouring the internet for stats.

Fastball Percentage

Our fastball percentage (FB%) statistic measures how frequently a pitcher throws a pitch classified as a "fastball," measured as a percentage of overall pitches thrown. We qualify three types of fastballs:

1. The traditional four-seam fastball;
2. The two-seam fastball or sinker;
3. "Hard cutters," which are pitches that have the movement profile of a cut fastball and are used as the pitcher's primary offering or in place of a more traditional fastball.

For example, a pitcher with a FB% of 67 throws any combination of these three pitches about two-thirds of the time.

Whiff Rate

Everybody loves a swing and a miss, and whiff rate (WHF) measures how frequently pitchers induce a swinging strike. To calculate WHF, we add up all the pitches thrown that ended with a swinging strike, then divide that number by a pitcher's total pitches thrown. Most often, high whiff rates correlate with high strikeout rates (and overall effective pitcher performance).

Called Strike Probability

Called Strike Probability (CSP) is a number that represents the likelihood that all of a pitcher's pitches will be called a strike while controlling for location, pitcher and batter handedness, umpire and count. Here's how it works: on each pitch, our model determines how many times (out of 100) that a similar pitch was called for a strike given those factors mentioned above, and when normalized for each batter's strike zone. Then we average the CSP for all pitches thrown by a pitcher in a season, and that gives us the yearly CSP percentage you see in the stats boxes.

As you might imagine, pitchers with a higher CSP are more likely to work in the zone, where pitchers with a lower CSP are likely locating their pitches outside the normal strike zone, for better or for worse.

Projections

Many of you aren't turning to this book just for a look at what a player has done, but for a look at what a player is going to do: the PECOTA projections. PECOTA, initially developed by Nate Silver (who has moved on to greater fame as a political analyst), consists of three parts:

1. Major-league equivalencies, which use minor-league statistics to project how a player will perform in the major leagues;
2. Baseline forecasts, which use weighted averages and regression to the mean to estimate a player's current true talent level; and
3. Aging curves, which uses the career paths of comparable players to estimate how a player's statistics are likely to change over time.

With all those important things covered, let's take a look at what's in the book this year.

Team Prospectus

You bought this book to learn more about your favorite (or maybe least-favorite, who are we to judge?) team, so let's talk about them. After a thoughtful preview of the 2019 season, you'll be presented with our Team Prospectus. This outlines many of the key statistics for each team's 2018 season, as well as a very inviting stadium diagram.

First you'll find the Performance Graphs page. The first is the 2018 Hit List Ranking. This shows our Hit List Rank for the team on each day of the 2018 season and is intended to give you a picture of the ups and downs of the team's season, including their highest and lowest ranks of the year. Hit List Rank measures overall team performance and drives the Hit List Power Rankings at the baseballprospectus.com website.

The second graph is Committed Payroll and helps you see how the team's payroll has compared to the MLB and divisional average payrolls over time. Payroll figures are currents as of January 1, 2019; with so many free agents still unsigned as of this writing, the final 2018 figure will likely be significantly different for many teams. (In the meantime, you can always find the most current data at Baseball Prospectus' Cot's Baseball Contracts page.)

New York Yankees 2019

The third graph is Farm System Ranking and displays how the Baseball Prospectus prospect team has ranked the organization's farm system since 2007. It also indicates the highest and lowest ranks that the farm system achieved over that time.

We start the Team Performance page with the squad's unadjusted and third-order 2018 win-loss records, presented in divisional context. We then list the three highest performing hitters and pitchers by WARP for 2018. Beneath that are a host of other team statistics. **Pythag** presents an adjusted 2018 winning percentage, calculated by taking runs scored per game (**RS/G**) and runs allowed per game (**RA/G**) for the team, and running them through a version of Bill James' Pythagorean formula that was refined and improved by David Smyth and Brandon Heipp. (The formula is called "Pythagenpat," which is equally fun to type and to say.)

Next up is **DRC+**, described earlier, to indicate the overall hitting ability of the team either above or below league-average. Run prevention on the pitching side is covered by **DRA** (also mentioned earlier) and another metric: Fielding Independent Pitching (**FIP**), which calculates another ERA-like statistic based on strikeouts, walks, and home runs recorded. Defensive Efficiency Rating (**DER**) tells us the percentage of balls in play turned into outs for the team, and is a quick fielding shorthand that rounds out run prevention.

After that, we have several measures related to roster composition, as opposed to on-field performance. **B-Age** and **P-Age** tell us the average age of a team's batters and pitchers, respectively. **Salary** is the combined team payroll for all on-field players, and Doug Pappas' Marginal Dollars per Marginal Win (**M$/MW**) tells us how much money a team spent to earn production above replacement level.

Ending this batch of statistics is the number of disabled list days a team had over the season (**DL Days**) and the amount of salary paid to players on the disabled list (**$ on DL**); this final number is expressed as a percentage of total payroll.

Next to each of these stats, we've listed each team's MLB rank in that category from 1st to 30th. In this, 1st always indicates a positive outcome and 30th a negative outcome, except in the case of salary–1st is highest.

The Team Projections page is intended to convey the team's operational capacity entering the 2019 season. We start with the team's PECOTA projected record for 2019, again in divisional context. The **+/-** column indicates how many more or less wins the team is projected to get than they got in 2018. We then list the three highest projected hitters and pitchers by WARP for 2018. A brief farm system summary follows, with the team's top prospect and number of BP Top 101 Prospects. Finally, we list the key new players and departed players, along with their 2019 projected WARP.

Alex Bregman 3B

Born: 03/30/94 Age: 25 Bats: R Throws: R
Height: 6'0" Weight: 180 Origin: Round 1, 2015 Draft (#2 overall)

YEAR	TEAM	LVL	AGE	PA	R	2B	3B	HR	RBI	BB	K	SB	CS	AVG/OBP/SLG
2016	CCH	AA	22	285	54	16	2	14	46	42	26	5	3	.297/.415/.559
2016	FRE	AAA	22	83	17	6	0	6	15	5	12	2	1	.333/.373/.641
2016	HOU	MLB	22	217	31	13	3	8	34	15	52	2	0	.264/.313/.478
2017	HOU	MLB	23	626	88	39	5	19	71	55	97	17	5	.284/.352/.475
2018	HOU	MLB	24	705	105	51	1	31	103	96	85	10	4	.286/.394/.532
2019	HOU	MLB	25	675	96	38	3	23	78	73	107	12	4	.272/.359/.463

Breakout: 6% Improve: 52% Collapse: 5% Attrition: 2% MLB: 100%
Comparables: Anthony Rendon, David Wright, Pablo Sandoval

YEAR	TEAM	LVL	AGE	PA	DRC+	VORP	BABIP	BRR	FRAA	WARP
2016	CCH	AA	22	285	172	38.9	.286	1.6	SS(51): -3.4, 3B(11): 1.4	2.7
2016	FRE	AAA	22	83	161	10.0	.333	-1.2	SS(14): 2.1, LF(3): -0.1	0.8
2016	HOU	MLB	22	217	107	9.6	.317	0.5	3B(40): 0.9, SS(6): -0.1	1.1
2017	HOU	MLB	23	626	114	34.7	.311	-1.5	3B(132): 8.7, SS(30): -2.9	3.9
2018	HOU	MLB	24	705	150	72.6	.289	-1.6	3B(136): 5.4, SS(28): -0.4	7.4
2019	HOU	MLB	25	675	125	37.3	.295	0.0	3B 7, SS 0	4.6

After the projections page, we share a few items about the team's home ballpark. There's the aforementioned diagram of the park's dimensions (including distances to the outfield wall), a few important biographical facts about the stadium, a graphic showing the height of the wall from the left-field pole to the right-field pole, and a table showing three-year park factors for the stadium. The park factors are displayed as indexes where 100 is average, 110 means that the park inflates the statistic in question by 10 percent, and 90 means that the park deflates the statistic in question by 10 percent.

Following the ballpark page, we have a **Personnel** section that lists many of the important decision-makers and upper-level field and operations staff members for the franchise, as well as any former Baseball Prospectus staff members who are currently part of the organization.

Position Players

After all that information and a thoughtful bylined essay covering each team, we present our player comments. Each player is listed with the major-league team who employed him as of early January 2019. If a player changed teams after that point via free agency, trade, or any other method, you'll be able to find them in the book for their previous squad.

First, we cover biographical information (age is as of June 30, 2019) before moving onto the stats themselves. Our statistic columns include standard identifying information like **YEAR**, **TEAM**, **LVL** (level of affiliated play) and **AGE** before getting into the numbers. Next, we provide raw, unstranslated numbers like you might find on the back of your dad's baseball cards: **PA** (plate appearances), **R** (runs), **2B** (doubles), **3B** (triples), **HR** (home runs), **RBI** (runs batted in), **BB** (walks), **K** (strikeouts), **SB** (stolen bases) and **CS** (caught stealing). Then we have unadjusted "slash" statistics: **AVG** (batting average), **OBP** (on-base percentage) and **SLG** (slugging percentage).

Just below the stats box is **PECOTA** data, which is discussed further in a following section. After that, it's on to a pithy and always-informative comment written by a member of the Baseball Prospectus staff, before we cover more stats.

The second text box repeats YEAR, TEAM, LVL, AGE, and PA, then moves on to **DRC+** (Deserved Runs Created Plus), which we described earlier as total offensive expected contribution compared to the league average. Next, one of our oldest active metrics, **VORP** (Value Over Replacement Player), considers offensive production, position and plate appearances. In essence, it is the number of runs contributed beyond what a replacement-level player at the same position would contribute if given the same percentage of team plate appearances. VORP does not consider the quality of a player's defense.

BABIP (batting average on balls in play) tells us how often a ball in play fell for a hit, and can help us identify whether a batter may have been lucky or not ... but note that high BABIPs also tend to follow the great hitters of our time, as well as speedy singles hitters who put the ball on the ground.

The next item is **BRR** (Baserunning Runs), which covers all of a player's baserunning accomplishments which includes (but isn't limited to) swiped bags and failed attempts. Next is **FRAA** (Fielding Runs Above Average), which also includes the number of games previously played at each position noted in parentheses. Multi-position players have only their two most frequent positions listed here, but their total FRAA number reflects all positions played.

Our last column here is **WARP** (Wins Above Replacement Player). WARP estimates the total value of a player, which means for hitters it takes into account hitting runs above average (calculated using the DRC+ model), BRR and FRAA. Then, it makes an adjustment for positions played and gives the player a credit for plate appearances based upon the difference between "replacement level"--which is derived from the quality of players added to a team's roster after the start of the season--and the league average.

Catchers

Catchers are a special breed, and thus they have earned their own separate box which displays some of the defensive metrics that we've built just for them. As an example, let's check out J.T. Realmuto.

YEAR	TEAM	P. COUNT	FRM RUNS	BLK RUNS	THRW RUNS	TOT RUNS
2016	MIA	18935	-8.5	1.8	2.1	-5.6
2017	MIA	18959	5.3	1.7	1.0	9.1
2018	MIA	16399	-0.4	0.9	0.1	0.4
2019	PHI	18448	-1.4	1.5	0.7	0.8

The **YEAR** and **TEAM** columns match what you'd find in the other stat box. **P. COUNT** indicates the number of pitches thrown while the catcher was behind the plate, including swinging strikes, fouls, and balls in play. **FRM RUNS** is the total run value the catcher provided (or cost) his team by influencing the umpire to call strikes where other catchers did not. **BLK RUNS** expresses the total run value above or below average for the catcher's ability to prevent wild pitches and passed balls. **THRW RUNS** is calculated using a similar model as the previous two statistics, and it measures a catcher's ability to throw out basestealers but also to dissuade them from testing his arm in the first place. It takes into account factors like the pitcher (including his delivery and pickoff move) and baserunner (who could be as fast as Billy Hamilton or as slow as Yonder Alonso). **TOT RUNS** is the sum of all of the previous three statistics.

Pitchers

Let's give our pitchers a turn, using 2018 NL Cy Young winner Jacob deGrom as our example. Take a look at his first stat block: the first line and the **YEAR**, **TEAM**, **LVL** and **AGE** columns are the same as in the position player example earlier.

Here too, we have a series of columns that display raw, unadjusted statistics compiled by the pitcher over the course of a season: **W** (wins), **L** (losses), **SV** (saves), **G** (games pitched), **GS** (games started), **IP** (innings pitched), **H** (hits allowed) and **HR** (home runs allowed). Next we have two statistics that are rates: **BB/9** (walks per nine innings) and **K/9** (strikeouts per nine innings), before returning to the unadjusted **K** (strikeouts).

Next up is **GB%** (ground ball percentage), which is the percentage of all batted balls that were hit in the ground, including both outs and hits. Remember, this is based on observational data and subject to human error, so please approach this with a healthy dose of skepticism.

BABIP (batting average on balls in play) is calculated using the same methodology as it is for position players, but it often tells us more about a pitcher than it does a hitter. With pitchers, a high BABIP is often due to poor defense or bad luck, and can often be an indicator of potential rebound, and a low BABIP may be cause to expect performance regression. (A typical league-average BABIP is close to .290-.300.)

After a witty 150ish words on the player like only Baseball Prospectus's staff can provide, it's on to that second stat block, which repeats the YEAR, TEAM, LVL, and AGE columns. The metrics **WHIP** (walks plus hits per inning pitched) and **ERA**

New York Yankees 2019

(earned run average) are old standbys: WHIP measures walks and hits allowed on a per-inning basis, while ERA measures earned runs on a nine-inning basis. Neither of these stats are translated or adjusted.

DRA (Deserved Run Average) was described at length earlier, and measures how many runs the pitcher "deserved" to allow per nine innings. Please note that since we lack all the data points that would make for a "real" DRA for minor-league events, the DRA displayed for minor league partial-seasons is based off of different data. (That data is a modified version of our cFIP metric, which you can find more information about on our website.)

Jacob deGrom   RHP
Born: 06/19/88   Age: 31   Bats: L   Throws: R
Height: 6'4"   Weight: 180   Origin: Round 9, 2010 Draft (#272 overall)

YEAR	TEAM	LVL	AGE	W	L	SV	G	GS	IP	H	HR	BB/9	K/9	K	GB%	BABIP
2016	NYN	MLB	28	7	8	0	24	24	148	142	15	2.2	8.7	143	47%	.312
2017	NYN	MLB	29	15	10	0	31	31	201[1]	180	28	2.6	10.7	239	48%	.305
2018	NYN	MLB	30	10	9	0	32	32	217	152	10	1.9	11.2	269	48%	.281
2019	NYN	MLB	31	13	9	0	31	31	186	145	18	2.3	10.7	221	46%	.286

Breakout: 8%   Improve: 29%   Collapse: 28%   Attrition: 6%   MLB: 85%
Comparables: Erik Bedard, A.J. Burnett, CC Sabathia

YEAR	TEAM	LVL	AGE	WHIP	ERA	DRA	WARP	MPH	FB%	WHF	CSP
2016	NYN	MLB	28	1.20	3.04	3.30	3.5	96.3	59.6	12.1	47.2
2017	NYN	MLB	29	1.19	3.53	3.02	5.7	97.2	55.5	14.5	49.5
2018	NYN	MLB	30	0.91	1.70	2.09	8.0	98.2	52.1	16.3	48.4
2019	NYN	MLB	31	1.02	2.91	3.23	3.9	96.6	54.5	14.8	48.2

Just like with hitters, **WARP** (Wins Above Replacement Player) is a total value metric that puts pitchers of all stripes on the same scale as position players. We use DRA as the primary input for our calculation of WARP. You might notice that relief pitchers (due to their limited innings) may have a lower WARP than you were expecting or than you might see in other WARP-like metrics. WARP does not take leverage into account, just the actions a pitcher performs and the expected value of those actions ... which ends up judging high-leverage relief pitchers differently than you might imagine given their prestige and market value.

MPH gives you the pitcher's 95th percentile velocity for the noted season, in order to give you an idea of what the *peak* fastball velocity a pitcher possesses. Since this comes from our pitch tracking data, it is not publicly available for minor-league pitchers.

Finally, we display the three new pitching metrics we described earlier. **FB%** (fastball percentage) gives you the percentage of fastballs thrown out of all pitches. **WhiffRt** (whiff rate) tells you the percentage of swinging strikes induced out of all pitches. **CS Prob** (called strike probability) expresses the likelihood of all pitches thrown to result in a called strike, after controlling for factors like handedness, umpire, pitch type, count, and location.

PECOTA

All players have PECOTA projections for 2019, as well as a set of other numbers that describe the performance of comparable players according to PECOTA. All projections for 2019 are for the player at the date we went to press in early January and are projected into the league and park context as indicated by the team abbreviation. All PECOTA projected statistics represent a player's projected major-league performance.

The numbers beneath the player's stats—Breakout, Improve, Collapse, Attrition—are part and parcel of the PECOTA projections. They estimate the likelihood of changes in performance relative to the player's previously-established level of production, based on the performance of comparable players:

Breakout Rate is the percent change that a player's production will improve by at least 20 percent relative to the weighted average of his performance over his most recent seasons.

Improve Rate is the percent chance that a player's production will improve at all relative to his baseline performance. A player who is expected to perform just the same as he has in the recent past will have an Improve Rate of 50 percent.

Collapse Rate is the percent chance that a position player's production will decline by at least 25 percent relative to his baseline performance.

Attrition Rate operates on playing time rather than performance. Specifically, it measures the likelihood that a player's playing time will decrease by at least 50 percent relative to his established level.

Breakout Rate and Collapse Rate can sometimes be counterintuitive for players who have already experienced a radical change in performance level. It's also worth noting that the projected decline in a player's rate performances might not be indicative of an expected decline in underlying ability or skill, but could just be an anticipated correction following a breakout season.

MLB% is the percentage of similar players who played in the major leagues in their relevant season.

The final pieces of information are the player's three highest-scoring comparable players as determined by PECOTA. All comparables represent a snapshot of how the listed player was performing at the same age as the current player, so if a 23-year-old pitcher is compared to Bartolo Colon, he's actually being compared to a 23-year-old Colon, not the version that pitched for the Rangers in 2018, nor to Colon's career as a whole.

New York Yankees 2019

A few points about pitcher projections. First, we aren't yet projecting peak velocity, so that column will be blank in the PECOTA lines. Second, projecting DRA is trickier than evaluating past performance, because it is unclear how deserving each pitcher will be of his anticipated outcomes. However, we know that another DRA-related statistic–contextual FIP or cFIP–estimates future run scoring very well. So for PECOTA, the projected DRA figures you see are based on the past cFIPs generated by the pitcher and comparable players over time, along with the other factors described above.

Lineouts

In each chapter's Lineouts section, you'll find abbreviated text comments, as well as most of same information you'd find in our full player comments. We limit the stats boxes in this section to only including the 2018 information for each player.

Exclusive Player Visualizations

In our constant battle to provide you with new and interesting baseball content you can't find anywhere else, we've added a trio of data visualizations to each hitter's entry in these books and a pair of visualizations for each pitcher.

For hitters, you'll find three new infographics. The first is each player's **Batted Ball Distribution**, which displays the five major sections of the field: LF (left), LCF (left center), CF (center), RCF (right center), and RF (right). The percentage indicated tells us what percentage of batted balls from that hitter fell within that part of the field during the 2018 season. We've also included the hitter's slugging percentage on balls in play (also called **SLGCON**) for that part of the field.

You'll also see two heatmaps: **Strike Zone vs LHP** and **Strike Zone vs RHP**. These heat maps represent a view of the strike zone from behind the catcher. Areas where there is a darker coloration represent the places where a higher percentage of pitches resulted in hits. In other words, the heatmap represents a hitter's "sweet spots" for getting hits against either left-handed or right-handed pitchers, depending on the image.

Pitchers get two images that help explain what their pitches look like from a hitter's perspective: **Pitch Shape vs LHH** and **Pitch Shape vs RHH**. These images show you the shape and the "tunneling" effect of each pitcher's offerings from the batter's perspective. For each type of pitch that a pitcher throws (represented by an indicator shape), there's a set of dots indicating the flight path, where each dot represents a 0.01-second interval. This maps the average trajectory and speed of an offering, ending where the ball crosses the plate. The solid black box represents the regular strike zone, while the gray contour lines indicate the range of locations that a pitcher typically works in.

Below the image, we provide a bit more detailed information about each pitcher's average offering in the **Pitch Types** box. Here, we also list each of the pitcher's major offerings under the **Type** column.

- **Fastballs** (which usually refers to the four-seam variation)
- **Sinkers** and/or two-seam fastballs
- **Cutters** (which could include "hard" cutters like cut fastballs and "soft" cutters that resemble hard sliders)
- **Changeups** (not including most splitters)
- **Splitters** (split-fingered pitches, forkballs, and some split-changes)
- **Sliders** and/or slurves
- **Curveballs** (including spike-curveballs and knuckle-curveballs, as well as some slurvy curves)
- **Slow curveballs** and/or eephus pitches
- **Knuckleballs**
- **Screwballs**

The **Freq** column indicates the percentage of overall pitches that fall into each of those type categories; if a pitcher has a 16.55% score for changeups, then that's the percent of all pitches that he throws as changeups. **Velo** is exactly what you think it is: the average miles per hour for each pitch type. **H Mov** is the number of inches of horizontal movement on the average pitch of that type, while **V Mov** is the number of inches of vertical movement on the average pitch of that type. (At Baseball Prospectus, we measure this over the long flight of the ball and include gravity into the V Mov number in order to give you the most realistic representation of what the pitch *actually* does.)

If you're wondering about the second number in brackets, that's the index for that velocity or movement compared to the league average. Like DRC+, a score of 100 means that the speed or movement is about the same as league average, while a higher score means that there's higher velocity or movement than the league average. Numbers below 100 indicate less velocity or movement than the league average.

Part 1: Team Analysis

Table for Two: Previewing the 2019 New York Yankees

Derek Albin and E.J. Fagan

DEREK ALBIN: Is it safe to say that the Yankees are the AL East favorites this year? The Red Sox may have won 108 games and the World Series, but they're bringing back the same team along with a worse bullpen. Tampa Bay should prove they weren't a fluke but probably won't be a threat for the pennant. The Yankees definitely improved, even though the entire baseball universe was expecting them to make a big splash in free agency.

E.J. FAGAN: I was a little bit surprised to see the distance between PECOTA's win projection for the Yankees (96) and the Red Sox (89) and Rays (86). Boston was a truly historic powerhouse team last year, and are largely returning the same starting rotation and lineup. While the Yankees have added 5 or so wins in the rotation and bullpen, they also have to make up Didi Gregorius' production from last year. I'm not one to bet against PECOTA, but I'd be pretty comfortable taking the over on Boston's 89 wins.

Tampa is definitely a dark horse team, and I'd also take the over on 86 wins if forced to make a bet. I can't help but look at good-but-not-great projections for players like Tommy Pham (2.3 WARP), Kevin Kiermaier (2.8 WARP) and Joey Wendle (2.0 WARP) and expect that someone has a career year and adds 3 wins on top of that. They also are taking lots of small bets on guys like Ji-Man Choi, Austin Meadows, Avisail Garcia, Yandy Diaz, and others who could break out. If they add a strong lineup to their incredible pitching staff, they could be as good as the Yankees or Red Sox.

Now that we're talking about breakouts, the Yankees have a bunch of interesting candidates. Who do you think is the best bet to break out in 2019?

DEREK: Can we consider Luke Voit a breakout candidate? I'm hesitant because his baseline PECOTA hitting projection is great (128 DRC+). It makes him almost too easy of a choice.

Otherwise, I have my money on Clint Frazier. The most important thing is that he's now free and clear of the concussion symptoms that mostly ruined his 2018. Plus, it's not like he took a step back when he was ostensibly healthy last year. He tore up Triple-A pitching (140 DRC+) despite the lingering symptoms. If that's a sign of things to come, he should be able to wrestle away the starting left field job from Brett Gardner at some point this season. Gardner was pretty terrible down the stretch last summer.

PECOTA doesn't think Frazier is the next baby bomber though. Obviously I'm taking the over on his forecasted 85 DRC+. Do you agree, or do you have someone else you're eyeing to take a big leap forward?

E.J.: I completely agree with you on Clint Frazier. PECOTA doesn't know that he suffered post-concussion symptoms all season.

I don't know whether to predict a Gleyber Torres breakout, or declare that it already happened and we're about to see him contribute for a full season. Torres was worth 3.7 WARP in 123 games, or almost a 5-win pace. However, he was even hotter early in the season before his July injury and rushed return from the disabled list, with a .331/.381/.602 batting line on June 1st. I don't think he will be that good, but he definitely has room to improve on his 120 DRC+.

DEREK: Let's go to the other end of the spectrum now. Is there anyone you foresee taking a nosedive? I think I know who you're going to say, so I don't want to steal your thunder. Instead, I'll go with Brett Gardner.

Gardner has been a first half player his entire career, but I think this is finally the season that he isn't strong out of the gate. He was so, so bad to finish last year and basically lost his job to Andrew McCutchen. I'm actually surprised that PECOTA still likes Gardner so much: it forecasts 2.2 WARP and a 98 DRC+ in only 472 plate appearances. I know his defense is still exceptional, but I just don't see him as a useful bat anymore. Not after a career worst xwOBA of .290 last year.

E.J.: Neither I nor the Yankees are counting on Gardner next year, so in a sense I think you're right. At the same time, I think he could maintain a decent per-game performance next year. Throughout his 30s, Gardner has broken down in the second half nearly every year. If he's rested, I think he could still be productive.

It pains me to say this, but the correct answer is Miguel Andujar. Andujar's outcomes were pretty good for a rookie, 120 DRC+, 2 WARP. He hit the ball all over the field for power. Unfortunately, the inputs were much worse. Statcast put his xwOBA at .323. PECOTA is projecting a 1 WARP season in 2019. Andujar gets great contact, but his plate discipline and defense are going to have to improve if he is going to be a consistently valuable major league player. I don't see any indication that either is going to get better, so he better hope that his batted ball luck doesn't regress. He needs to slug around .500 to be worth playing on a championship team. I hope that I'm wrong.

Andujar was one of the last prospects to be called up from the previous era of the Yankee farm system. Now that they've graduated so many great players, the minor league system is entering a new phase. Even so, there are a few players that we could see this year. Who do you think will make an impact?

DEREK: Yeah, the prospect turnover has resulted in the system being pretty skewed toward guys who are further away. There are still some guys who lost their prospect status but haven't really had a chance to make an impact yet, like Clint Frazier and Tyler Wade.

If we're talking strictly prospect eligible, it's basically only pitchers who have any shot at contributing in the majors this year. The first guy that comes to mind is the team's top prospect: Jonathan Loaisiga. He's definitely in line for a few starts this season after a respectable debut last summer. However, he might have a better chance to make a dent as a reliever, at least for this season.

If Michael King's elbow discomfort isn't overly serious, he has a great chance to soak up innings as a spot starter. He seemingly came out of nowhere last summer, and now is on the cusp of the big leagues.

A couple of other guys I'd like to mention are Trevor Stephan and Deivi Garcia. Both are starters (for now), but they have the stuff to pitch important innings out of the bullpen. I guess I shouldn't disregard Chance Adams even though he took a big step back last year. He needs his stuff to come back, though. Otherwise, he might wind up in the bullpen, which wouldn't be the end of the world.

I want to circle back to your pessimism about Andujar for a second. I don't think we can avoid the elephant in the room any longer: Manny Machado. The Yankees made a handful of nice moves this offseason, but it feels like a let down because they passed on Machado. Even if Andujar is good, the odds of him being Machado-good are slim to none. I know the Yankees made some nice moves this offseason, such as the James Paxton and Adam Ottavino pickups, but it's hard not to find this offseason underwhelming. Are they going to regret not signing Machado (or Bryce Harper for that matter)?

E.J.: Yes. Money isn't any good if you don't spend it, but the best spending opportunities only come once every few years. The Yankees had a chance to buy out the prime years of one of the best players in baseball. So far, they have declined. I think they will regret it pretty quickly.

I think about signings like this in opportunity cost terms. If you spend a bunch of money today, you lose the ability to spend that money tomorrow. Who do the Yankees sacrifice by signing Manny Machado? There are no mid-20s free agent stars set to hit the market over the next two seasons. Even if the Yankees want to go after Mike Trout during the 2020-2021 offseason, they will have well over $70 million in expiring contracts to clear payroll room.

Here's how I predict this saga plays out: the Yankees pass on Machado. Andujar plays more like a 1-win player than a 3-win player, or is at least bad enough on defense that they move him to another position. The Yankees realize they need a better player at third base, and go out and sign Nolan Arenado to a similar deal, but he'll be three years older. The Yankees get burned by their short-sightedness.

DEREK: And that's only if Arenado doesn't wind up signing and extension to stay in Colorado, which seems very possible. Then again, even if Arenado hits the open market, could we really trust the Yankees to spend? Based on recent behavior, I think the answer is no. There's always another excuse to be found.

E.J.: Of course, the true winners of this sage will be the Steinbrenner family, who will continue to maintain the exact same payroll level as they have for a decade even as revenues soar.

Assuming the Yankees don't suddenly sign Machado, we've already talked about PECOTA's 95-win projection. How many do you think they win in the intend?

DEREK: I'll say 100, the same as last year. I know that's aggressive, but I think it's going to be driven by two things: their competition and Giancarlo Stanton. There are a bunch of terrible teams in the American League, including their divisional foe from Baltimore which will be the worst team in baseball yet again. Plus, even though Boston has a great team, they sat on their hands this winter. As for Stanton, I think year two is going to be a monster year. I know I'm not alone in feeling this way, but I can see an MVP-caliber campaign. Maybe we get a redux of A-Rod's 2005, which was also his second season in pinstripes.

What say you?

E.J.: I think the Yankees do a little better than PECOTA, largely on the strength of Aaron Hicks and Gleyber Torres. 98 wins.

Performance Graphs

2018 Hit List Ranking

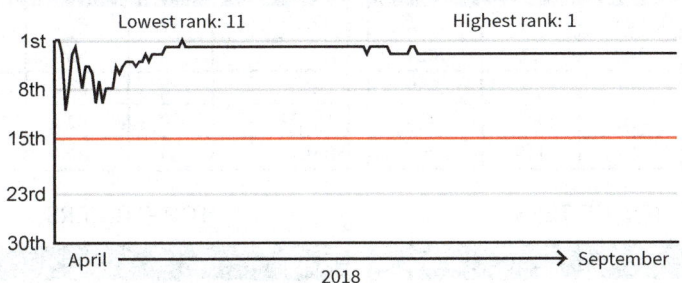

Committed Payroll (in millions)

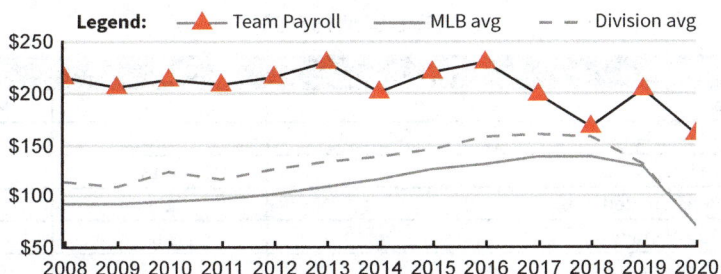

Farm System Ranking

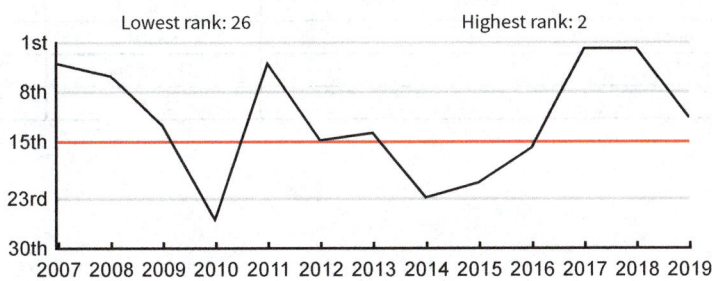

2018 Team Performance

ACTUAL STANDINGS

Team	W	L	Pct
BOS	108	54	.666
NYA	**100**	**62**	**.617**
TBA	90	72	.555
TOR	73	89	.450
BAL	47	115	.290

THIRD-ORDER STANDINGS

Team	W	L	Pct
NYA	**99**	**63**	**.611**
BOS	99	63	.611
TBA	98	64	.604
TOR	70	92	.432
BAL	54	108	.333

TOP HITTERS

Player	WARP
Aaron Judge	4.7
Didi Gregorius	4.4
Gleyber Torres	3.7

TOP PITCHERS

Player	WARP
Luis Severino	5.6
Masahiro Tanaka	2.5
Dellin Betances	2.1

VITAL STATISTICS

Statistic Name	Value	Rank
Pythagenpat	.612	4th
Runs Scored per Game	5.25	2nd
Runs Allowed per Game	4.13	10th
Deserved Runs Created Plus	108	4th
Deserved Run Average	3.80	4th
Fielding Independent Pitching	3.66	3rd
Defensive Efficiency Rating	.700	22nd
Batter Age	27.2	6th
Pitcher Age	28.7	17th
Salary	$166.1M	7th
Marginal $ per Marginal Win	$3.0M	21st
Disabled List Days	$1,283.0M	20th
$ on DL	19%	20th

2019 Team Projections

PROJECTED STANDINGS

Team	W	L	Pct	+/-
NYA	**96**	**66**	**.592**	**-4**
BOS	90	72	.555	-18
TBA	85	77	.524	-5
TOR	76	86	.469	+3
BAL	57	105	.351	+10

TOP PROJECTED HITTERS

Player	WARP
Aaron Judge	4.9
Giancarlo Stanton	4.1
Gary Sanchez	3.4

TOP PROJECTED PITCHERS

Player	WARP
James Paxton	3.8
Luis Severino	3.4
Masahiro Tanaka	2.9

FARM SYSTEM REPORT

Top Prospect	Number of Top 101 Prospects
Jonathan Loaisiga, #64	2

KEY DEDUCTIONS

Player	WARP
Andrew McCutchen	2.5
Neil Walker	1.8
Lance Lynn	1.6
Sonny Gray	1.4
Adeiny Hechavarria	0.9
David Robertson	0.8
Justus Sheffield	0.7

KEY ADDITIONS

Player	WARP
James Paxton	3.8
DJ LeMahieu	2.9
Adam Ottavino	0.7

Team Personnel

General Manager
Brian Cashman

SVP, Assistant General Manager
Jean Afterman

Assistant General Manager
Michael Fishman

VP, Baseball Operations
Tim Naehring

Manager
Aaron Boone

Yankee Stadium Stats

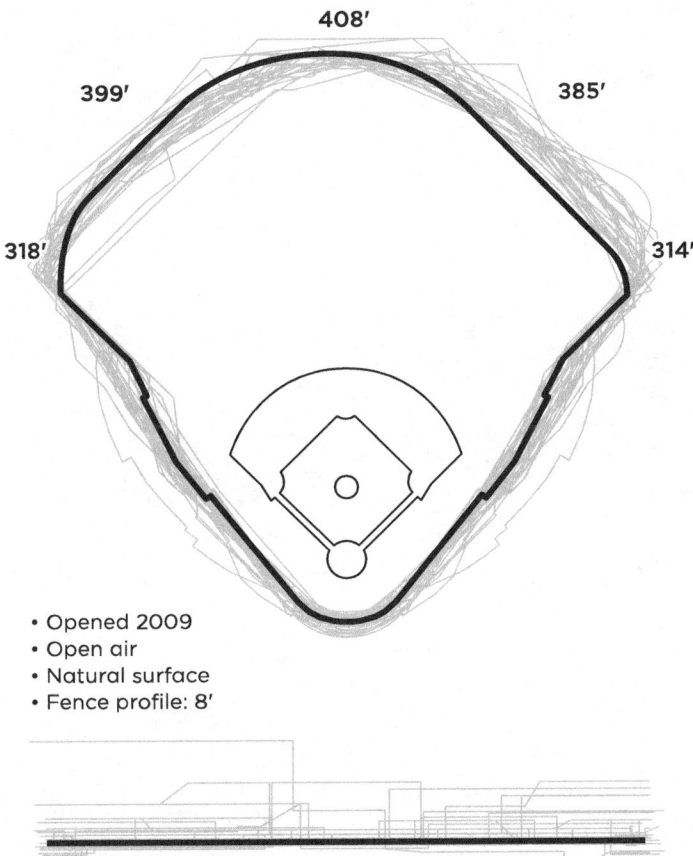

- Opened 2009
- Open air
- Natural surface
- Fence profile: 8'

Three-Year Park Factors

Runs	Runs/RH	Runs/LH	HR/RH	HR/LH
103	104	102	112	118

Yankees Team Analysis

The current era of Yankees baseball, one in which a young team is led by a young manager, can be traced back to October 2005. The Yankees were one year removed from their embarrassing 2004 ALCS loss to the Red Sox and they'd just been ousted in the 2005 ALDS in five games by the Angels. Their top two starters in that series were 36-year-old Mike Mussina and 41-year-old Randy Johnson. Hall of Fame talents, both of them, but past their prime, like so many other Yankees. That way of doing business would soon end.

Following that 2005 ALDS loss general manager Brian Cashman signed a contract extension—he leveraged interest from the post-Ed Wade Phillies into a nice raise—after receiving assurances from George Steinbrenner that he would have autonomy over the baseball operations. Cashman didn't get it (no general manager truly has 100 percent autonomy), but he did get considerably more power, and he used it to overhaul the front office and ramp up the team's analytic and pro scouting efforts. He would begin to build the team in his image.

That's when the Yankees went from being the Evil Empire with a monster payroll to being a smart team with a monster payroll. Their farm system and player development improved, bolstered by improved drafting and prolific spending in the international market. They identified buy-low types and hit the jackpot with Nick Swisher, Didi Gregorius, and Aaron Hicks. The Yankees have had some high-profile misses since then (see: Ellsbury, Jacoby), but the spend spend spend team-building philosophy has been replaced by homegrown stars and shrewd pickups. The 2017 season ended a game short of the World Series, but it was clear: The *Yankees*, as a concept, were back.

And, in 2018, they handed the keys to this burgeoning modern baseball powerhouse over to a rookie manager. The successful and widely respected Joe Girardi was let go following the team's ALCS loss in 2017, and, soon after it was announced Girardi would not return, chairman Hal Steinbrenner said the managerial change would've been made even if the Yankees went to the World Series. Ouch. Girardi's fate had been decided long in advance.

To replace Girardi the Yankees hired Aaron Boone straight out of the broadcast booth. Boone spent 13 years in the big leagues from 1997-2009—he hit a rather notable home run in pinstripes, it's sometimes told—and had been in the broadcast booth since 2010. His brother, father, and grandfather were all big leaguers, but Boone had zero professional coaching or managerial experience. A team on the rise and in the game's largest market had just put a zero-experience manager in charge. To call it risky would be an understatement.

"Obviously, experience is very valuable and should be a check mark for somebody," Boone said during his introductory press conference. "But I would also say that I've been preparing for this job my entire life. I'm 44 years old now. I've been going to the ballpark since I was three and four years old. Going into broadcasting, I feel like so much of my job in the booth, especially the last few years, I find myself managing games all the time and thinking about strategies and thinking about situations."

Once Spring Training opened, Boone talked the talk. He talked about not having set bullpen roles and instead using guys like David Robertson, Chad Green, and Dellin Betances interchangeably. He talked about batting Aaron Judge leadoff to take advantage of his on-base skills. He talked about increased aggressiveness on the basepaths and treating the bench as an extension of the starting lineup rather than a bunch of dudes who only played when a regular needed a day. Boone appeared to be the platonic ideal of a saber-friendly manager.

A funny thing happened once the regular season started, however. Almost none of that stuff happened, and Boone and Girardi were damn near indistinguishable in terms of on-field strategy. Their lineups looked similar, which meant Brett Gardner in the leadoff spot even when better options (Hicks) existed, Judge married to the No. 2 spot, and using a lefty to break up a long string of right-handed batters (and vice versa) even if it meant using someone higher in the lineup than his production warranted. (Gregorius was often sandwiched between Judge and Giancarlo Stanton.)

That also meant fairly rigid bullpen roles. With Aroldis Chapman locked in at closer, Betances took over the eighth inning and Robertson was the primary seventh inning reliever. Green pitched in fifth and sixth inning situations, which arose quite often because, like Girardi, Boone rarely pushed his starting pitchers deep into the game. Only 35 times did a Yankees starter throw 100 pitches in a game in 2018, the 18th most in baseball. For years, they'd been consistently in the middle of the pack or below.

Girardi was often praised for his bullpen management and deservedly so. Year in and year out, the Yankees had a top flight bullpen under his watch. Girardi was also predictable with his regular season bullpen usage. He had set seventh and eighth inning relievers and rarely deviated. He also avoided using his relievers on back-to-back days whenever possible. In 2016 the Yankees had the ninth fewest instances of a reliever pitching on zero's day rest and they were a handful of games away from being bottom five. In 2017 they had the second fewest. Under Boone in 2018, they had the fifth fewest and were two games away from the third fewest.

Then there's the rest. Lordy, there's the rest. Every day around 3:30 p.m. ET is lineup complaining o'clock on social media. (It's that way for every team, but the Yankees have a larger social media presence than most, so yeah.) The daily lineup gets posted and the complaints begin. Why is that guy hitting so low? Why is that guy sitting a day after hitting a home run? Why is that guy in the lineup against a lefty? On and on it goes. The energy of those capable of nitpicking the lineup—the lineup of a great and high-scoring offense, at that—on a daily basis is admirable. It takes persistence.

The daily auditors could take note of at least one phenomenon. Stanton did something in 2018 no Yankee had done since Robinson Cano wore pinstripes: He played in 157 games. One-hundred-and-fifty-eight, to be exact. No other Yankee played in that many games over the last five seasons. There are lots of reasons for that (injuries, poor performance, etc.), including New York's apparent dedication to resting their regular position players. And in their case, that means predetermined rest. This guy is going to sit this day no matter what, even if he goes 3-for-4 with two homers the night before. The Yankees are big on rest, and have been for a few years. Fans hate it, as the lineup complainers remind us daily, but the Yankees believe in it.

The Yankees replaced a successful longtime veteran manager in Girardi with a neophyte in Boone and...nothing changed. At least not in terms of regular season strategy. Boone did have some noticeable gaffes in the postseason, no doubt about it. Most notably, he had too long a leash with Luis Severino and CC Sabathia in Games 3 and 4 of the ALDS, respectively, and he also brought Lance Lynn into a bases loaded, no outs situation in Game 3 rather than a high-strikeout guy like Robertson or Betances. Big mistakes, those were. Rookie mistakes? It's certainly seems that way. It's hard to imagine Girardi doing something like that, at least not toward the end of his tenure.

Despite those high-profile mishaps, not a whole lot changed on the field with the switch from Girardi to Boone. Almost nothing changed, really. The lineup was built the same way. The bullpen was used the same way when it came to defined roles and rest. Starters weren't pushed deep into games. Position players sat on predetermined days. Take a step back and examine things from high above, and it's awfully tough to look at the 2018 Yankees and the 2014-17 or so Yankees and see a meaningful difference in managerial strategy. Girardi and Boone were carbon copies.

That leads to two natural questions. One, why the managerial change then? Cashman cited communication issues when the Yankees announced Girardi would not return and, if nothing else, Boone is a great talker and very personable. He is several orders of magnitude more skilled at dealing with the media—no small thing in New York—and the Yankees believed he could foster better relationships with the players, particularly the young up-and-coming guys like Judge and Severino and Gleyber Torres. That's why the change was made. To improve what happens behind closed doors in the clubhouse, on the plane, at the hotel, etc.

And two, if the on-field strategy is the same across two managers, who's really calling the shots? Is it all one giant coincidence that Girardi and Boone managed the same team exactly the same way? It's possible, but it seems incredibly unlikely. Chances are the directives are coming from upstairs, from the front office. It's no secret front offices, specifically analytical staffs, are more involved in the day-to-day operations across baseball than ever before. They provide data and information, and it's up to the manager and coaches to digest it and disseminate it. Some players like data. Others hate it. It's up to the manager and coaching staff to provide that individual touch and make best use of the information.

Front offices have been giving the coaching staff data for literally decades. The data is more sophisticated now, and better tailored to the recipient, but they've been doing it a long time. The next logical step in the analytical takeover is the front office weighing in on specific moves and strategies. We all read Moneyball, right? We all remember Billy Beane telling Art Howe to use Chad Bradford in high-leverage spots. The Yankees appear to have taken that a step further. This is the lineup construction we want. These are the bullpen roles we want. Rest these players on these days. So on and so forth. These directives, assuming they do actually exist, have remained in place across managers.

Teams across baseball are hiring younger, less experienced managers. The Yankees took it to the extreme with Boone, but the Phillies hired Gabe Kapler, the Mets hired Mickey Callaway, the Reds hired David Bell, and the Twins hired Rocco Baldelli, among others. Teams are hiring inexperienced managers en masse in part because they can develop them into the type of manager they want. Veteran skippers like Buck Showalter and Bruce Bochy and Bob Melvin are adaptable, they have to be to stick around as long as they have, but they're also set in their ways to some degree. Guys like Boone are not. They are a ball of managerial clay that can molded into whatever the front office wants in their dugout leader.

There are always going to be individual moves that stand out as different—again, few could see any way Girardi passes over Robertson or Green to go to Lynn with the bases loaded and no outs in a postseason game—but the overarching themes are the same. Strategically, the Yankees were very similar under Boone in 2018 as they were under Girardi in 2017 and earlier. The differences show up in the clubhouse, and in the way the information from Cashman's front office is used. It's been over a decade since Cashman was ostensibly given autonomy over the baseball operations. Now the fruits of that labor are extending into the dugout more than ever before. ■

—*Mike Axisa is a writer at cbssports.com.*

Part 2: Player Analysis

Miguel Andujar 3B

Born: 03/02/95 Age: 24 Bats: R Throws: R
Height: 6'0" Weight: 215 Origin: International Free Agent, 2011

YEAR	TEAM	LVL	AGE	PA	R	2B	3B	HR	RBI	BB	K	SB	CS	AVG/OBP/SLG
2016	TAM	A+	21	251	34	10	2	10	41	18	30	1	3	.283/.343/.474
2016	TRN	AA	21	319	28	16	2	2	42	21	42	2	1	.266/.323/.358
2017	TRN	AA	22	272	30	23	1	7	52	12	38	2	3	.312/.342/.494
2017	SWB	AAA	22	250	36	13	1	9	30	17	33	3	0	.317/.364/.502
2017	NYA	MLB	22	8	0	2	0	0	4	1	0	1	0	.571/.625/.857
2018	NYA	MLB	23	606	83	47	2	27	92	25	97	2	1	.297/.328/.527
2019	NYA	MLB	24	562	68	29	2	22	73	33	92	2	1	.271/.319/.462

Breakout: 9% Improve: 56% Collapse: 7% Attrition: 15% MLB: 95%
Comparables: Cheslor Cuthbert, Edwin Encarnacion, Lonnie Chisenhall

Life during the George Steinbrenner era meant that any young player was always viewed with suspicion. Even when the highly-touted Derek Jeter was set to begin 1996 with the team, Steinbrenner infamously demanded to swap Mariano Rivera for a soon-to-be-retired Felix Fermin. It's still shocking to see prospect after prospect get a chance over the last three years, and even more shockingly, seeing Miguel Andujar announced as the starting third baseman sight unseen. All things considered, what a success it was. He broke Joe DiMaggio's Yankees record for doubles by a rookie, while putting up a .298 batting average and .855 OPS over 149 games. His performance will still be seen through fan double-vision. Older fans will probably see the player they wished was around more often in today's game—gap power, hitting for average, and a relatively low strikeout rate. Other analytically-inclined fans wince at the statuesque range at third. What that means for his future is up in the air. While the bat will carry him, will it be at third, which a certain free agent acquisition would complicate? Or at first, complicated by Luke Voit and extra offensive demands? It's difficult to succeed as one-half of a ballplayer, but that's often more of a rookie ballplayer than other teams can claim.

YEAR	TEAM	LVL	AGE	PA	DRC+	VORP	BABIP	BRR	FRAA	WARP
2016	TAM	A+	21	251	132	14.6	.289	0.0	3B(51): 4.1	1.4
2016	TRN	AA	21	319	83	12.3	.296	0.5	3B(64): -2.6	-0.3
2017	TRN	AA	22	272	125	19.2	.338	-1.6	3B(58): -4.5	0.4
2017	SWB	AAA	22	250	138	20.3	.333	0.3	3B(57): -1.4	1.4
2017	NYA	MLB	22	8	96	2.0	.571	0.0	3B(3): 0.0	0.0
2018	NYA	MLB	23	606	120	38.1	.316	-0.1	3B(136): -15.2	2.0
2019	NYA	MLB	24	562	106	17.4	.290	-0.9	3B -8	0.8

Miguel Andujar, continued

Batted Ball Distribution

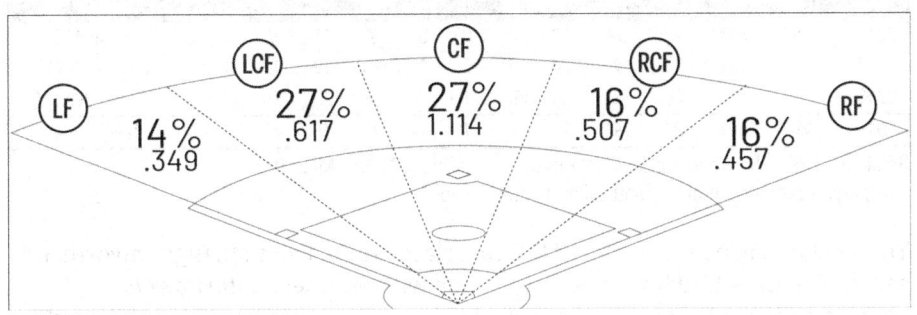

Strike Zone vs LHP   **Strike Zone vs RHP**

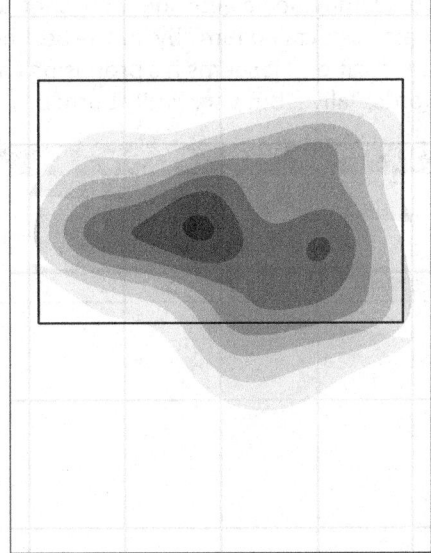

Greg Bird 1B

Born: 11/09/92 Age: 26 Bats: L Throws: R
Height: 6'4" Weight: 220 Origin: Round 5, 2011 Draft (#179 overall)

YEAR	TEAM	LVL	AGE	PA	R	2B	3B	HR	RBI	BB	K	SB	CS	AVG/OBP/SLG
2017	SWB	AAA	24	59	12	4	0	3	7	11	9	0	0	.298/.424/.574
2017	NYA	MLB	24	170	20	7	0	9	28	19	42	0	0	.190/.288/.422
2018	NYA	MLB	25	311	23	16	1	11	38	30	78	0	0	.199/.286/.386
2019	NYA	MLB	26	192	22	9	1	6	22	18	45	0	0	.229/.309/.400

Breakout: 10% Improve: 56% Collapse: 7% Attrition: 10% MLB: 94%
Comparables: Adam LaRoche, Matt LaPorta, Mike Jacobs

Though he may be the owner of the cat related to Dr. Evil's Mr. Bigglesworth, it seems that Greg Bird has more in common with another *Austin Powers* character—Mustafa, who was responsible for Bigglesworth's hairless fate and had his chair collapsed from underneath him into a flaming dungeon. Bird may not be in a dungeon but he is riding the bench, losing a starting spot to Luke Voit after hitting to just a .327 wOBA from June 1st until the trade deadline. One would imagine he gets one more shot considering Brian Cashman, though three years past, called him "by far the best hitter (among prospects) in the organization," it seems his promising career in the Bronx is, in Mustafa's own words, "alive, but very badly burned."

YEAR	TEAM	LVL	AGE	PA	DRC+	VORP	BABIP	BRR	FRAA	WARP
2017	SWB	AAA	24	59	156	4.7	.306	-1.0	1B(10): 0.9	0.3
2017	NYA	MLB	24	170	99	1.2	.194	-1.0	1B(46): -1.1	0.0
2018	NYA	MLB	25	311	84	-7.7	.230	-1.8	1B(74): 1.4	-0.2
2019	NYA	MLB	26	192	87	0.0	.273	-0.4	1B 0	0.0

Greg Bird, continued

Batted Ball Distribution

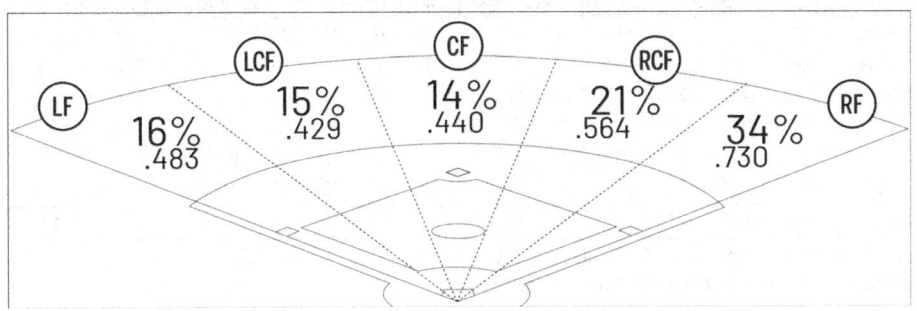

Strike Zone vs LHP   **Strike Zone vs RHP**

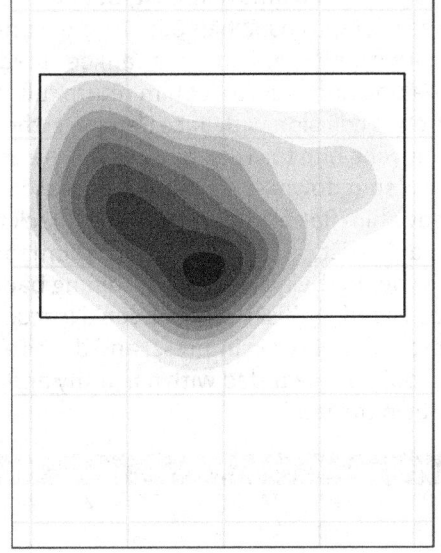

Clint Frazier OF

Born: 09/06/94   Age: 24   Bats: R   Throws: R
Height: 6'1"   Weight: 190   Origin: Round 1, 2013 Draft (#5 overall)

YEAR	TEAM	LVL	AGE	PA	R	2B	3B	HR	RBI	BB	K	SB	CS	AVG/OBP/SLG
2016	AKR	AA	21	391	56	25	1	13	48	41	86	13	4	.276/.356/.469
2016	SWB	AAA	21	108	17	2	3	3	7	7	30	0	0	.228/.278/.396
2017	SWB	AAA	22	320	46	19	2	12	42	37	69	9	2	.256/.344/.473
2017	NYA	MLB	22	142	16	9	4	4	17	7	43	1	0	.231/.268/.448
2018	NYA	MLB	23	41	9	3	0	0	1	5	13	0	0	.265/.390/.353
2018	SWB	AAA	23	216	38	14	3	10	21	23	52	4	2	.311/.389/.574
2019	NYA	MLB	24	210	25	11	1	8	25	18	55	3	1	.234/.305/.431

Breakout: 11%   Improve: 43%   Collapse: 19%   Attrition: 25%   MLB: 81%
Comparables: Derek Fisher, Lewis Brinson, Joe Benson

Chronic Traumatic Encephalopathy, commonly known as CTE, has been studied for nearly a century, and yet the implications of head injuries in baseball haven't been in team and fan lexicon for more than a decade or so. This is evident not only in how teams handle it, but how open players are in speaking up about their symptoms. When Clint Frazier suffered a concussion from a wall collision during spring training, the Yankees made sure to carefully inch him along, waiting until July to let him return full-time. After suffering migraines resulting from a collision with Jace Peterson, the Yankees once again shut him down, allowing him to creep back, this time as far as a minor league rehab stint. He was shut down—again—and his season was complete. Even though Michael Kay gave him flak for this, hearkening back to a time when that concussion lexicon didn't exist, saying, "Shame on [him] for not getting healthy." No one can blame Frazier for being frustrated, sniping back a "#ShameOnYouBro," especially considering this has truly been a lost season. Lost year or not, he is still a top prospect who can impress, and despite the grumbles, fans and Frazier alike should be rewarded with a healthy and concussion-free Red Lightning years down the road.

YEAR	TEAM	LVL	AGE	PA	DRC+	VORP	BABIP	BRR	FRAA	WARP
2016	AKR	AA	21	391	123	24.2	.331	1.4	RF(31): -0.4, LF(26): 2.2	1.6
2016	SWB	AAA	21	108	74	1.6	.294	0.8	LF(13): -0.7, RF(6): 1.5	-0.1
2017	SWB	AAA	22	320	117	14.9	.291	1.8	LF(38): 1.2, RF(29): -1.3	1.0
2017	NYA	MLB	22	142	82	1.0	.307	0.8	LF(30): -3.1, RF(7): 0.4	-0.2
2018	NYA	MLB	23	41	76	0.6	.429	0.2	LF(9): -0.7, CF(1): -0.2	-0.1
2018	SWB	AAA	23	216	140	20.4	.380	0.9	CF(26): -2.9, LF(16): -0.3	1.0
2019	NYA	MLB	24	210	88	3.5	.277	0.1	LF 0, RF 0	0.2

Clint Frazier, continued

Batted Ball Distribution

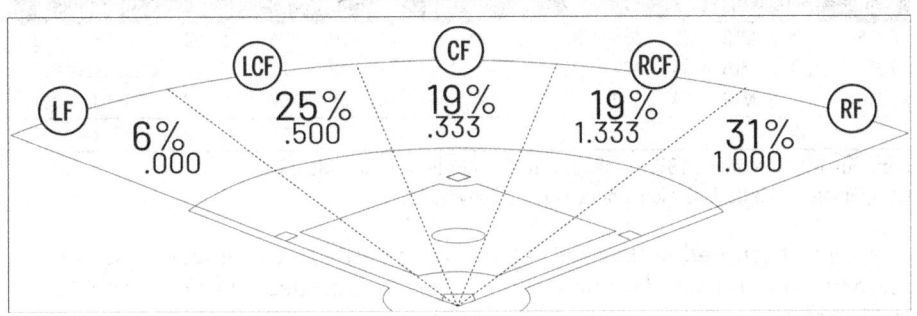

Strike Zone vs LHP　　　**Strike Zone vs RHP**

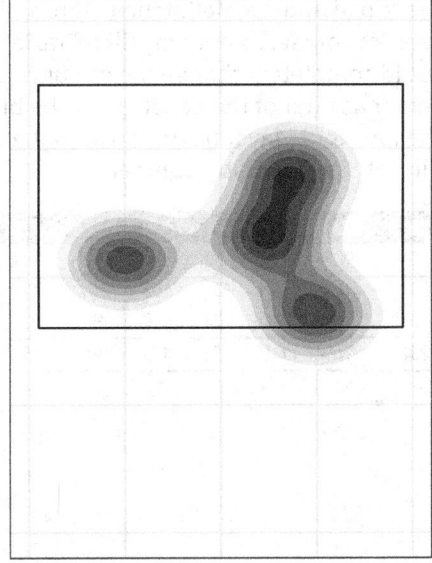

Brett Gardner LF

Born: 08/24/83 Age: 35 Bats: L Throws: L
Height: 5'11" Weight: 195 Origin: Round 3, 2005 Draft (#109 overall)

YEAR	TEAM	LVL	AGE	PA	R	2B	3B	HR	RBI	BB	K	SB	CS	AVG/OBP/SLG
2016	NYA	MLB	32	634	80	22	6	7	41	70	106	16	4	.261/.351/.362
2017	NYA	MLB	33	682	96	26	4	21	63	72	122	23	5	.264/.350/.428
2018	NYA	MLB	34	609	95	20	7	12	45	65	107	16	2	.236/.322/.368
2019	NYA	MLB	35	476	55	20	4	10	51	47	87	13	3	.262/.342/.401

Breakout: 0% Improve: 18% Collapse: 16% Attrition: 18% MLB: 74%
Comparables: Charlie Jamieson, Chone Figgins, Tony Gonzalez

The longest-tenured Yankee will get one more year as that namesake, as the team bought him out of his final contract year and settled on a one year, $7.5 million contract. By this point, Gardner is more fan favorite than useful player, as crazy as that may have sounded a year ago. Not long departed from his first 20/20 season, the markings of age and decline dominate the stat sheet. He hit just .209 in the second half with three home runs, and lost his everyday job to the trio of Andrew McCutchen, Aaron Hicks, and Aaron Judge. He still has his uses, of course, as not only Clint Frazier's future is in flux but a single injury could completely change the calculus. But as Gritty Gutty Gardner likely ends his career as rider of the bench, it will be bittersweet to see him in pinstripes not as the four-tool player he once was, but as a symbol of a bygone era where he himself was the Baby Bomber.

YEAR	TEAM	LVL	AGE	PA	DRC+	VORP	BABIP	BRR	FRAA	WARP
2016	NYA	MLB	32	634	93	14.8	.310	5.2	LF(147): 14.3, CF(3): -0.1	3.0
2017	NYA	MLB	33	682	107	25.7	.300	1.4	LF(122): 12.5, CF(22): 0.2	3.8
2018	NYA	MLB	34	609	90	12.3	.272	4.1	LF(107): 11.8, CF(34): 0.0	2.6
2019	NYA	MLB	35	476	95	15.3	.299	1.6	LF 8, CF -3	2.0

Brett Gardner, continued

Batted Ball Distribution

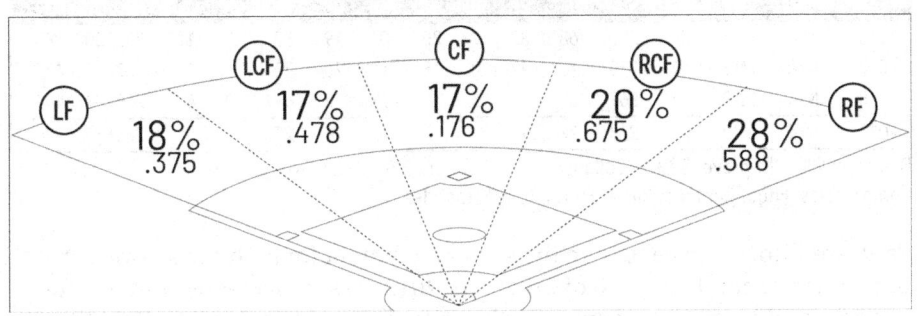

Strike Zone vs LHP   Strike Zone vs RHP

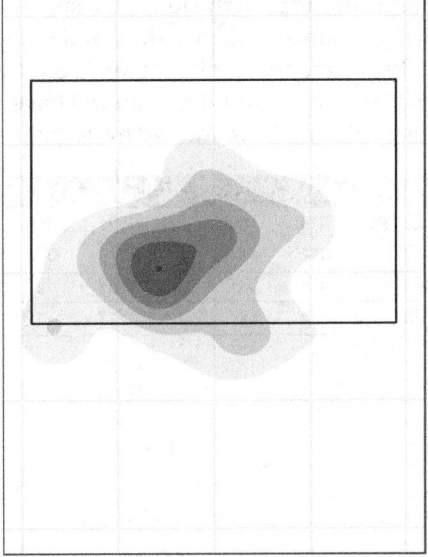

Didi Gregorius SS
Born: 02/18/90 Age: 29 Bats: L Throws: R
Height: 6'3" Weight: 205 Origin: International Free Agent, 2007

YEAR	TEAM	LVL	AGE	PA	R	2B	3B	HR	RBI	BB	K	SB	CS	AVG/OBP/SLG
2016	NYA	MLB	26	597	68	32	2	20	70	19	82	7	1	.276/.304/.447
2017	NYA	MLB	27	570	73	27	0	25	87	25	70	3	1	.287/.318/.478
2018	NYA	MLB	28	569	89	23	5	27	86	48	69	10	6	.268/.335/.494
2019	NYA	MLB	29	217	27	11	1	8	29	14	29	3	1	.283/.333/.470

Breakout: 9%   Improve: 52%   Collapse: 7%   Attrition: 5%   MLB: 96%
Comparables: Edgar Renteria, Rafael Furcal, Tony Fernandez

Very rarely does one get to pen the Annual comment for multiple seasons at once, but it seems like much of Gregorius' 2019 season is already written. After undergoing Tommy John surgery on his throwing hand on October 17th, the verdict was that he could return any time between June and August. It couldn't happen to a more exciting player: Of all of the stars of the new-look Baby Bombers, no one is a fan favorite quite like Gregorius. Not only he is one of the best shortstops in the league, a stellar defender with newly found power, but his array of dances, handshakes, and emoji-laden post-victory tweets help differentiate this Yankees team from the straight-laced teams of yore. His body will be missed, and the team will have to scramble to fill the performance. But the soul? That'll be missed more than anything.

YEAR	TEAM	LVL	AGE	PA	DRC+	VORP	BABIP	BRR	FRAA	WARP
2016	NYA	MLB	26	597	100	26.8	.290	4.2	SS(153): -5.6	2.5
2017	NYA	MLB	27	570	115	39.0	.287	1.9	SS(135): 4.9	4.4
2018	NYA	MLB	28	569	121	40.9	.259	2.3	SS(132): 0.4	4.4
2019	NYA	MLB	29	217	112	12.8	.294	-0.1	SS 0	1.2

Didi Gregorius, continued

Batted Ball Distribution

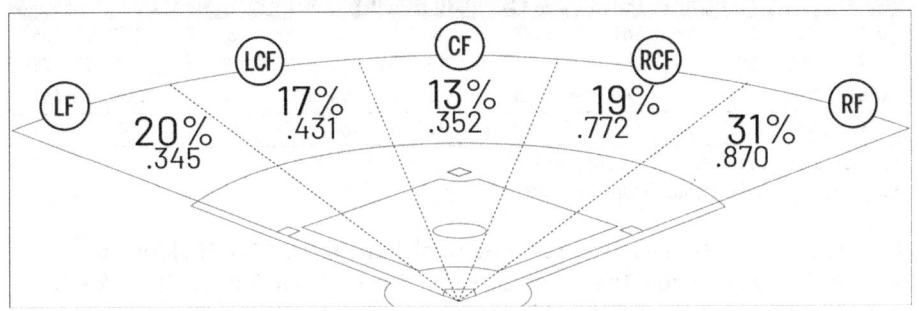

Strike Zone vs LHP   **Strike Zone vs RHP**

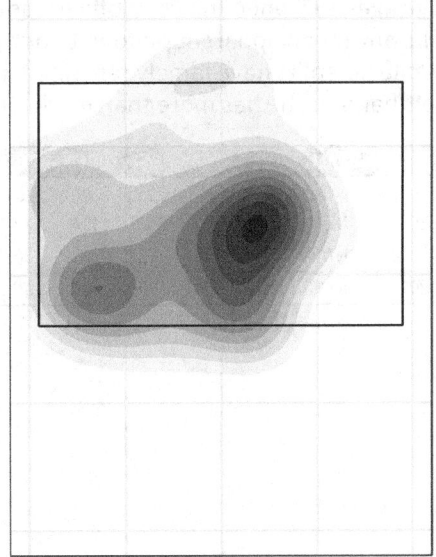

Aaron Hicks CF

Born: 10/02/89   Age: 29   Bats: B   Throws: R
Height: 6'1"   Weight: 202   Origin: Round 1, 2008 Draft (#14 overall)

YEAR	TEAM	LVL	AGE	PA	R	2B	3B	HR	RBI	BB	K	SB	CS	AVG/OBP/SLG
2016	NYA	MLB	26	361	32	13	1	8	31	30	68	3	4	.217/.281/.336
2017	NYA	MLB	27	361	54	18	0	15	52	51	67	10	5	.266/.372/.475
2018	NYA	MLB	28	581	90	18	3	27	79	90	111	11	2	.248/.366/.467
2019	NYA	MLB	29	525	75	22	2	19	60	63	99	10	4	.256/.350/.439

Breakout: 5%   Improve: 50%   Collapse: 12%   Attrition: 12%   MLB: 98%
Comparables: David DeJesus, Shane Victorino, Jon Jay

If your average baseball fan were asked to pick the ten best outfielders in baseball last year, would they even consider Aaron Hicks? You could make the argument that he's close to cracking the top five, as he set career records in home runs (27), walk percentage (15.5%), and conversely, strikeouts (111). His defense may have soured just a bit, ticking down six outs (3 to -3) in Statcast's Outs Above Average, but he has more than made up for that in power. It feels like ages ago when the front office was questioned for giving up John Ryan Murphy for an apparent platoon bench bat, but they've since been vindicated. While his splits have largely remained intact, still showing a weak spot against left-handers, he has more than made up in overall performance.

YEAR	TEAM	LVL	AGE	PA	DRC+	VORP	BABIP	BRR	FRAA	WARP
2016	NYA	MLB	26	361	79	-6.8	.248	0.3	RF(86): -0.7, LF(25): 2.7	0.3
2017	NYA	MLB	27	361	114	22.1	.290	2.0	CF(52): -0.8, LF(22): 0.8	1.8
2018	NYA	MLB	28	581	121	36.5	.264	2.3	CF(131): -8.6	2.9
2019	NYA	MLB	29	525	111	30.2	.286	0.2	CF -7	2.1

Aaron Hicks, continued

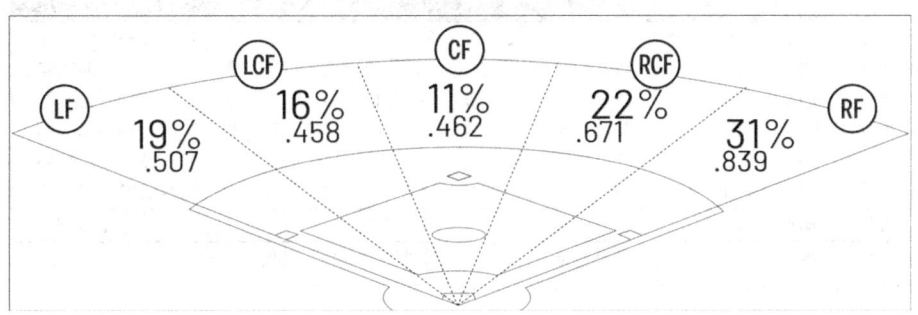

Batted Ball Distribution

Strike Zone vs LHP   Strike Zone vs RHP

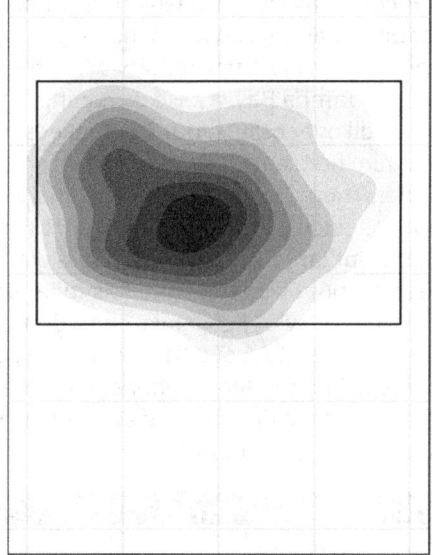

Kyle Higashioka C

Born: 04/20/90   Age: 29   Bats: R   Throws: R
Height: 6'1"   Weight: 205   Origin: Round 7, 2008 Draft (#230 overall)

YEAR	TEAM	LVL	AGE	PA	R	2B	3B	HR	RBI	BB	K	SB	CS	AVG/OBP/SLG
2016	TRN	AA	26	256	31	15	0	11	51	26	42	0	1	.293/.355/.509
2016	SWB	AAA	26	160	24	9	0	10	30	12	31	0	1	.250/.306/.514
2017	NYA	MLB	27	20	2	0	0	0	0	2	6	0	0	.000/.100/.000
2017	SWB	AAA	27	57	5	4	0	2	11	4	7	0	0	.264/.316/.453
2018	SWB	AAA	28	211	16	10	1	5	22	17	44	2	0	.202/.276/.346
2018	NYA	MLB	28	79	6	2	0	3	6	6	16	0	0	.167/.241/.319
2019	NYA	MLB	29	37	4	2	0	1	4	3	9	0	0	.206/.270/.353

Breakout: 9%   Improve: 20%   Collapse: 4%   Attrition: 19%   MLB: 45%
Comparables: Stephen Vogt, Dustin Garneau, Brett Nicholas

One usually doesn't think of the Yankees when they consider sabermetric advances, but the franchise has always been on the hunt for pitch framing. Jose Molina may have been a statistical oddity when he was on Tampa Bay, a case of valuing that skill over others, but the Yankees had him first, and it's not like he was tearing the cover off the ball in New York either. There was Chris Stewart, who was mocked by fans for his abysmal bat but collected 21 framing runs in 2013, and had 6+ WARP over a three year stretch that went largely unnoticed. There was Francisco Cervelli, who could never stay healthy, but ultimately put up similar framing numbers in his first season in Pittsburgh. Kyle Higashioka shouldn't be forgotten, either. He had just a .583 OPS, but his CSAA of 0.013 implies he could still be valuable in an extended stretch, if he can lift his offense to at least forgettable levels. If someone in the Bronx is sprinkling framing and defense fairy dust, the front office is betting it takes effect in short order.

YEAR	TEAM	P. COUNT	FRM RUNS	BLK RUNS	THRW RUNS	TOT RUNS
2017	NYA	813	1.7	-0.1	0.0	1.5
2017	SWB	2153	4.3	-0.3	-0.1	3.8
2018	NYA	3384	3.2	0.8	-0.1	4.4
2018	SWB	6908	7.2	0.6	-0.2	7.6
2019	NYA	1439	1.0	0.0	-0.1	0.9

YEAR	TEAM	LVL	AGE	PA	DRC+	VORP	BABIP	BRR	FRAA	WARP
2016	TRN	AA	26	256	143	22.4	.305	-2.0	C(61): 12.2	3.0
2016	SWB	AAA	26	160	126	7.3	.252	-1.9	C(36): 4.2	1.2
2017	NYA	MLB	27	20	59	-1.7	.000	-0.1	C(8): 1.6	0.2
2017	SWB	AAA	27	57	105	2.3	.273	-0.2	C(14): 4.5	0.7
2018	SWB	AAA	28	211	61	-0.9	.234	-0.7	C(49): 6.6	0.4
2018	NYA	MLB	28	79	98	-2.6	.170	-0.7	C(27): 3.8	0.7
2019	NYA	MLB	29	37	65	0.1	.236	-0.1	C 1	0.1

Kyle Higashioka, continued

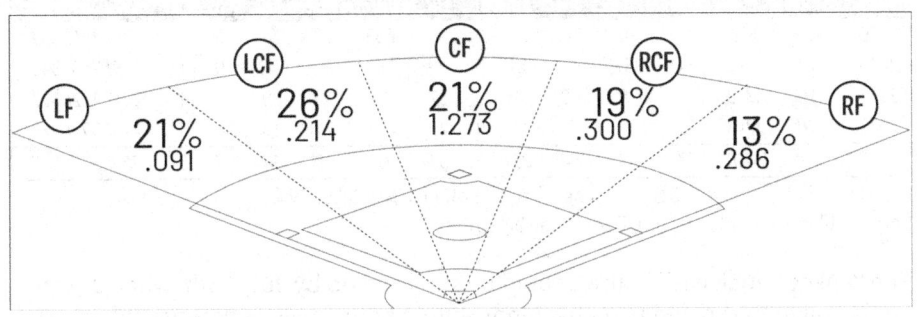

Strike Zone vs LHP

Strike Zone vs RHP

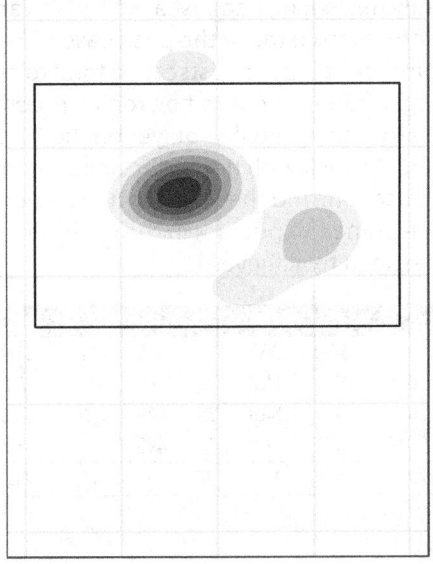

Aaron Judge RF

Born: 04/26/92   Age: 27   Bats: R   Throws: R
Height: 6'7"   Weight: 282   Origin: Round 1, 2013 Draft (#32 overall)

YEAR	TEAM	LVL	AGE	PA	R	2B	3B	HR	RBI	BB	K	SB	CS	AVG/OBP/SLG
2016	SWB	AAA	24	410	62	18	1	19	65	47	98	5	0	.270/.366/.489
2016	NYA	MLB	24	95	10	2	0	4	10	9	42	0	1	.179/.263/.345
2017	NYA	MLB	25	678	128	24	3	52	114	127	208	9	4	.284/.422/.627
2018	NYA	MLB	26	498	77	22	0	27	67	76	152	6	3	.278/.392/.528
2019	NYA	MLB	27	637	104	26	2	34	91	98	184	7	3	.259/.378/.509

Breakout: 2%   Improve: 55%   Collapse: 9%   Attrition: 0%   MLB: 99%
Comparables: Giancarlo Stanton, Darryl Strawberry, Jose Canseco

The Yankees' luck with injuries could be summed up by July 26th, when Jakob Junis drilled Aaron Judge on the ulnar styloid bone in his right wrist. What was expected to be a short DL stint dragged on until September 14th, and the team sagged, nearly losing their hold on the first wild card spot. If the team had not made the postseason then we'd probably be discussing whether his wrist was fully healed; he had just a .300 wOBA and one home run in September. Well, until they did make the postseason. He hit .421 in five games with three home runs, bringing his postseason total to seven in just 18 games. With that, the organization shouldn't be too worried that he's healthy, and he is still likely to be the most valuable player on the 2019 team. The Yankees' overall fortunes largely track with his performance, and if this past postseason was any indication, and the organization finally gets their other ducks in a row, then they are primed to put him in the position to achieve the playoff glory he seems destined to achieve.

YEAR	TEAM	LVL	AGE	PA	DRC+	VORP	BABIP	BRR	FRAA	WARP
2016	SWB	AAA	24	410	141	31.4	.319	2.8	RF(66): 19.6, LF(7): -0.7	4.2
2016	NYA	MLB	24	95	63	-2.5	.282	-0.5	RF(27): -3.2	-0.6
2017	NYA	MLB	25	678	166	68.5	.357	-0.1	RF(141): 4.4	7.5
2018	NYA	MLB	26	498	137	33.3	.368	1.0	RF(90): 12.6, CF(1): -0.1	4.7
2019	NYA	MLB	27	637	136	46.3	.328	-0.8	RF 4	4.9

Aaron Judge, continued

Batted Ball Distribution

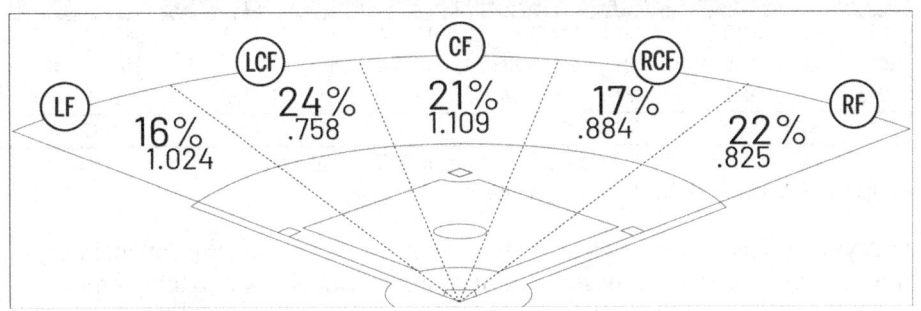

Strike Zone vs LHP   **Strike Zone vs RHP**

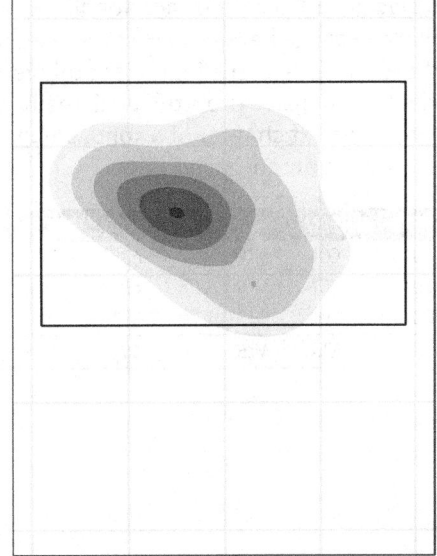

New York Yankees 2019

DJ LeMahieu 2B
Born: 07/13/88   Age: 30   Bats: R   Throws: R
Height: 6'4"   Weight: 215   Origin: Round 2, 2009 Draft (#79 overall)

YEAR	TEAM	LVL	AGE	PA	R	2B	3B	HR	RBI	BB	K	SB	CS	AVG/OBP/SLG
2016	COL	MLB	27	635	104	32	8	11	66	66	80	11	7	.348/.416/.495
2017	COL	MLB	28	682	95	28	4	8	64	59	90	6	5	.310/.374/.409
2018	COL	MLB	29	581	90	32	2	15	62	37	82	6	5	.276/.321/.428
2019	NYA	MLB	30	601	77	27	2	12	57	53	89	8	5	.288/.355/.413

Breakout: 4%   Improve: 47%   Collapse: 9%   Attrition: 11%   MLB: 96%
Comparables: Bobby Avila, Alex Cora, Jerry Lumpe

In days of yore, a guy like LeMahieu might set out into free agency off an injury-rattled "down" offensive season, rolling along on wheels that no longer moved down the track quickly enough to steal bases. The penalties would be exacerbated in the eyes of potential suitors by way of obedience to a vague Coors penalty, and we might be talking here about one-year contracts and the rebuilding of value. Unfortunately we're talking in vagaries because free agency is glacial and deadlines are deadlines. FRAA once again sniffed out a superior-to-all glove at the keystone. He produced among the league's best baserunning efforts, in spite of the inefficient thievery. And thanks to DRC+, we now know that the offensive drop-off, well, really wasn't much of a drop-off at all. He'll enter the next chapter of a solid, steady career as one of the better bets around to produce broad-based value.

YEAR	TEAM	LVL	AGE	PA	DRC+	VORP	BABIP	BRR	FRAA	WARP
2016	COL	MLB	27	635	124	44.1	.388	2.0	2B(146): -1.2	3.9
2017	COL	MLB	28	682	102	27.8	.351	3.4	2B(153): 20.5	4.7
2018	COL	MLB	29	581	98	17.2	.298	4.5	2B(128): 20.1	4.2
2019	NYA	MLB	30	601	109	27.5	.323	-0.9	2B 6, 3B 0	2.9

DJ LeMahieu, continued

Batted Ball Distribution

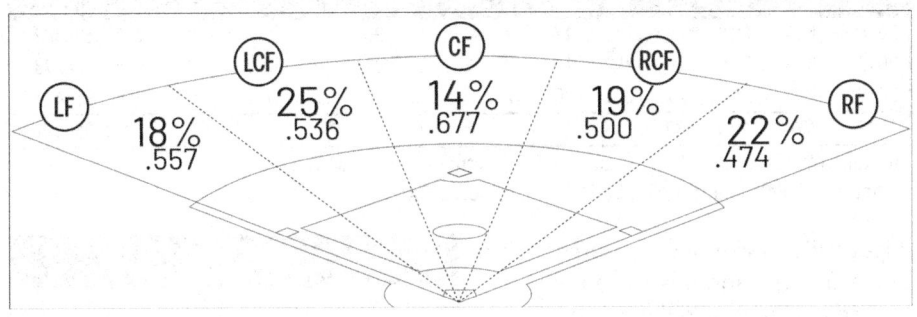

Strike Zone vs LHP **Strike Zone vs RHP**

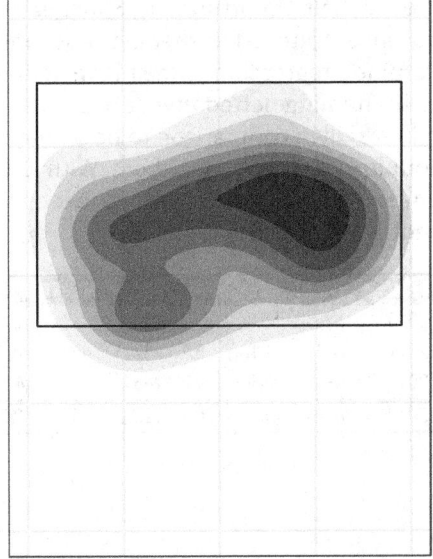

Austin Romine C

Born: 11/22/88   Age: 30   Bats: R   Throws: R
Height: 6'1"   Weight: 220   Origin: Round 2, 2007 Draft (#94 overall)

YEAR	TEAM	LVL	AGE	PA	R	2B	3B	HR	RBI	BB	K	SB	CS	AVG/OBP/SLG
2016	NYA	MLB	27	176	17	11	0	4	26	7	31	1	0	.242/.269/.382
2017	NYA	MLB	28	252	19	9	1	2	21	16	57	0	0	.218/.272/.293
2018	NYA	MLB	29	265	30	12	0	10	42	17	67	1	0	.244/.295/.417
2019	NYA	MLB	30	128	14	6	0	3	13	10	28	0	0	.241/.305/.371

Breakout: 6%   Improve: 47%   Collapse: 5%   Attrition: 31%   MLB: 77%
Comparables: Rob Johnson, Humberto Quintero, Jesus Sucre

Jazayerli's Law of Backup Catchers is a powerful one, and Austin Romine looked like he would live up to reaching .300, or at least a .300 OBP, for once after Gary Sanchez missed time, hitting .270 with an .825 OPS in the first half. Unfortunately, Sanchez's absence stretched further in the second half with a groin issue, and so did Romine's regression to the mean. It doesn't mean his value was null, of course, as his framing netted them about four runs or so, and his blocking, while a minor skill in comparison to how much the media focuses on it, gave them a couple of runs here and there. With just one more year of team control, which amusingly makes him one of the longest tenured Yankees, he will get one more shot at that magic .300 mark.

YEAR	TEAM	P. COUNT	FRM RUNS	BLK RUNS	THRW RUNS	TOT RUNS
2016	NYA	5754	-1.9	-0.1	-0.5	-2.7
2017	NYA	8705	6.3	-0.3	-1.3	4.3
2018	NYA	10341	4.2	2.2	0.0	6.3
2019	NYA	4956	1.7	0.2	-0.3	1.6

YEAR	TEAM	LVL	AGE	PA	DRC+	VORP	BABIP	BRR	FRAA	WARP
2016	NYA	MLB	27	176	81	-0.6	.271	-0.1	C(50): -3.2, 1B(6): -0.2	0.0
2017	NYA	MLB	28	252	66	-4.9	.277	-1.8	C(67): 4.5, 1B(12): 0.7	0.4
2018	NYA	MLB	29	265	85	4.5	.292	-3.1	C(76): 6.8	1.2
2019	NYA	MLB	30	128	83	2.7	.288	-0.2	C 1	0.4

Austin Romine, continued

Batted Ball Distribution

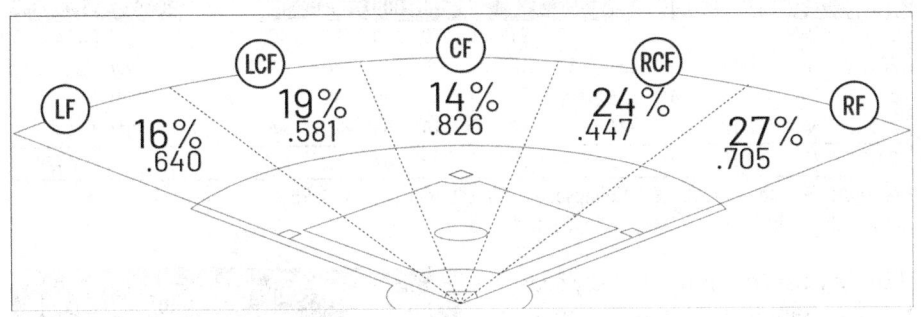

Strike Zone vs LHP   **Strike Zone vs RHP**

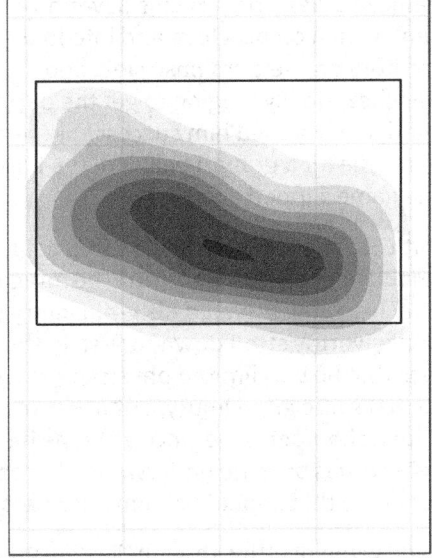

New York Yankees 2019

Gary Sanchez C
Born: 12/02/92   Age: 26   Bats: R   Throws: R
Height: 6'2"   Weight: 230   Origin: International Free Agent, 2009

YEAR	TEAM	LVL	AGE	PA	R	2B	3B	HR	RBI	BB	K	SB	CS	AVG/OBP/SLG
2016	SWB	AAA	23	313	39	21	1	10	50	21	45	7	1	.282/.339/.468
2016	NYA	MLB	23	229	34	12	0	20	42	24	57	1	0	.299/.376/.657
2017	NYA	MLB	24	525	79	20	0	33	90	40	120	2	1	.278/.345/.531
2018	NYA	MLB	25	374	51	17	0	18	53	46	94	1	0	.186/.291/.406
2019	NYA	MLB	26	595	78	27	1	29	87	55	130	3	1	.254/.333/.474

Breakout: 5%   Improve: 54%   Collapse: 6%   Attrition: 6%   MLB: 95%
Comparables: Buster Posey, Joey Votto, Travis d'Arnaud

YEAR	TEAM	P. COUNT	FRM RUNS	BLK RUNS	THRW RUNS	TOT RUNS
2016	NYA	5290	1.0	-1.4	1.2	1.2
2017	NYA	14363	7.4	-3.1	2.3	7.2
2018	NYA	10822	3.3	-4.3	0.2	-0.9
2018	SWB	560	0.0	0.0	0.0	0.4
2019	NYA	17787	7.1	-5.0	2.0	4.1

If there was a nadir in an lowly season for Gary Sanchez, it occurred on July 23rd. The Yankees were in Tampa playing the Rays, and two costly mistakes arguably cost them the game. A cross-up from Luis Severino sent a pitch off his glove and into foul territory on the third base side, and Sanchez, slowly jogging to get the ball, misjudged Jake Bauers heading around third and watched him successfully steal home. Then, in the last play of the game, he hit a ground ball with the bases loaded that he didn't hustle on, and the game slipped away.

With Sanchez, there's always that cold, hard, lived reality, and then an underlying, mitigating truth. The mitigating truth in this instance was that Sanchez re-aggravated his groin injury during the cross-up, explaining that cringeworthy stroll down to first. In the case of his season, the mitigating truth was that he was limited physically. Not only did he miss much of the season due to that same groin injury, but it was revealed that Sanchez had been dealing with a shoulder issue since 2017; he had one cortisone shot then, and after this season was over, he underwent a left shoulder debridement, with a treatment schedule that should get him back before Opening Day.

Even when healthy, though, it seems that fans can't get over one thing: passed balls. Sanchez had 18 passed balls in just 76 games caught, which obviously looks bad! But here's that underlying truth again: His ability to frame pitches canceled out the damage he did by letting them roll by. Sanchez is an ugly catcher, and also, quantifiably, a good catcher, a man designed to be roasted on sports radio and celebrated in person. The latter became evident at very end of the season, when Sanchez hit two monstrous home runs in Game Two of the ALDS at Fenway Park, the last one silencing the crowd with a bat drop, and he hit a fly ball in Game Four that, if launched one degree lower, would have sent the series to a winner-take-all. And that was with surgery pending.

Even with all of the trials and tribulations, both with injury and the press dogging him over passed balls, it's humorous that there is probably not a catcher you would take over him if you were to start a franchise today. That's a testament to talent that isn't going away, even if people don't always notice it.

YEAR	TEAM	LVL	AGE	PA	DRC+	VORP	BABIP	BRR	FRAA	WARP
2016	SWB	AAA	23	313	129	25.1	.302	-0.9	C(64): 10.8	3.0
2016	NYA	MLB	23	229	141	23.5	.317	-1.2	C(36): 1.4	2.1
2017	NYA	MLB	24	525	127	44.9	.304	2.3	C(104): 5.4, 1B(2): 0.0	4.9
2018	NYA	MLB	25	374	94	5.7	.197	-1.4	C(76): -1.4	1.1
2019	NYA	MLB	26	595	113	35.4	.281	-0.8	C 1	3.4

New York Yankees 2019

Gary Sanchez, continued

Batted Ball Distribution

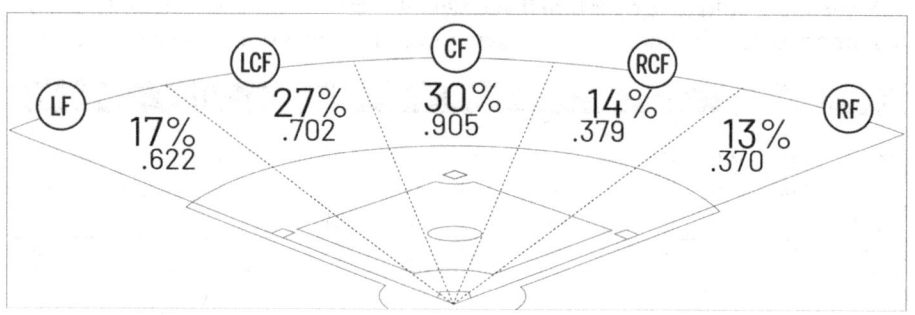

Strike Zone vs LHP   **Strike Zone vs RHP**

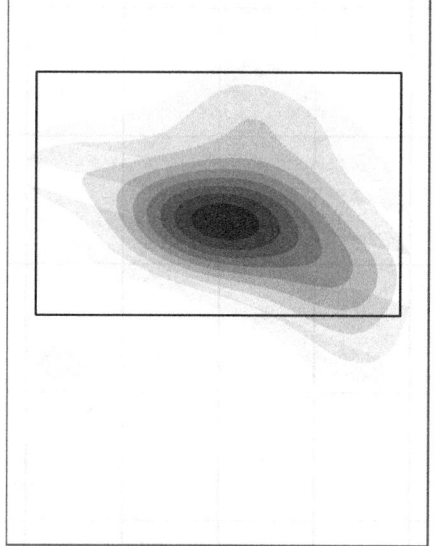

Giancarlo Stanton OF

Born: 11/08/89 Age: 29 Bats: R Throws: R
Height: 6'6" Weight: 245 Origin: Round 2, 2007 Draft (#76 overall)

YEAR	TEAM	LVL	AGE	PA	R	2B	3B	HR	RBI	BB	K	SB	CS	AVG/OBP/SLG
2016	MIA	MLB	26	470	56	20	1	27	74	50	140	0	0	.240/.326/.489
2017	MIA	MLB	27	692	123	32	0	59	132	85	163	2	2	.281/.376/.631
2018	NYA	MLB	28	705	102	34	1	38	100	70	211	5	0	.266/.343/.509
2019	NYA	MLB	29	651	95	28	1	38	106	78	175	3	1	.260/.355/.516

Breakout: 3%   Improve: 48%   Collapse: 5%   Attrition: 3%   MLB: 100%
Comparables: Fred McGriff, Dick Allen, Willie McCovey

The tone of Giancarlo Stanton's season will be forever tarred by his Yankee Stadium debut, where he went 0 for 5 with five strikeouts. He redeemed himself in other ways; while Aaron Judge missed time, Stanton himself largely carried the offense, offering a .384 wOBA with 22 home runs from June 1st to September 1st. Yankee fans may remember only the end, though, where he finished with a .316 wOBA in September and hit just .238 in the postseason with seven strikeouts. In the eyes of said fans, there will always be a paradox: They believe in spending money on the best players, but that well-paid players become complacent. Complacency or no (the answer: no), 2018 was a clear disappointment for the slugger. He set a career high in strikeouts, and his chase rate was the highest it's been in over five years. While he expected his more closed stance to be advantageous for Yankee Stadium, pitchers took advantage by beating him with heat up-and-in. There's no reason to worry yet, but for the Yankees to hoist another trophy, they need Stanton to return to his South Beach self.

YEAR	TEAM	LVL	AGE	PA	DRC+	VORP	BABIP	BRR	FRAA	WARP
2016	MIA	MLB	26	470	119	31.2	.290	0.4	RF(106): 2.4	2.4
2017	MIA	MLB	27	692	155	76.9	.288	-0.1	RF(149): 8.3	7.1
2018	NYA	MLB	28	705	117	30.1	.333	0.0	RF(37): -1.1, LF(36): 0.0	2.6
2019	NYA	MLB	29	651	134	42.0	.307	-0.9	LF -2, RF 1	4.1

Giancarlo Stanton, continued

Batted Ball Distribution

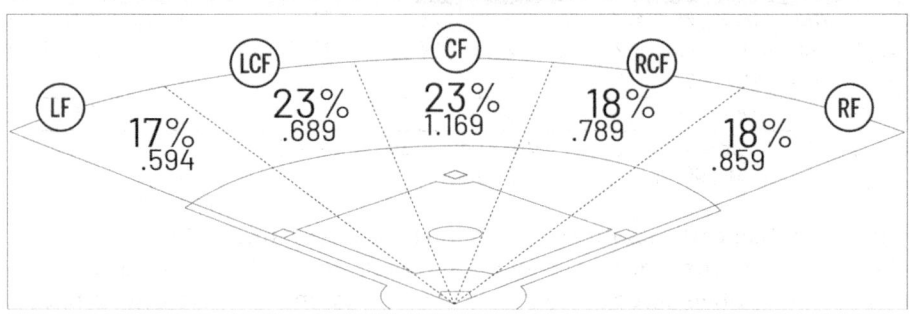

LF	LCF	CF	RCF	RF
17% .594	23% .689	23% 1.169	18% .789	18% .859

Strike Zone vs LHP

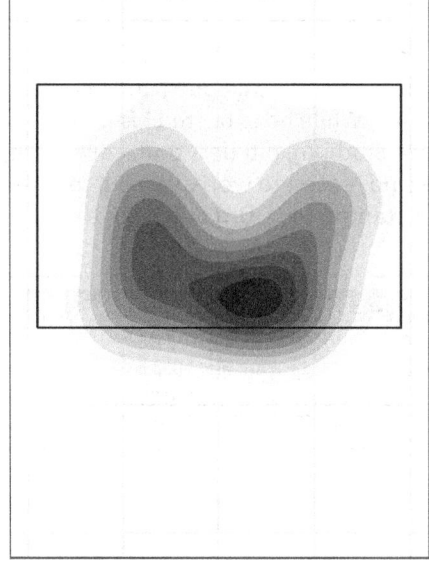

Strike Zone vs RHP

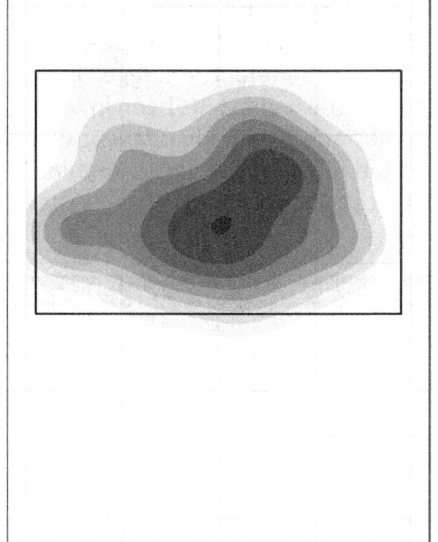

Gleyber Torres INF

Born: 12/13/96   Age: 22   Bats: R   Throws: R
Height: 6'1"   Weight: 200   Origin: International Free Agent, 2013

YEAR	TEAM	LVL	AGE	PA	R	2B	3B	HR	RBI	BB	K	SB	CS	AVG/OBP/SLG
2016	MYR	A+	19	409	62	23	3	9	47	42	87	19	10	.275/.359/.433
2016	TAM	A+	19	138	19	6	2	2	19	16	23	2	3	.254/.341/.385
2017	TRN	AA	20	139	22	10	1	5	18	17	21	5	4	.273/.367/.496
2017	SWB	AAA	20	96	9	4	1	2	16	13	26	2	2	.309/.406/.457
2018	SWB	AAA	21	56	6	3	1	1	11	5	10	1	1	.347/.393/.510
2018	NYA	MLB	21	484	54	16	1	24	77	42	122	6	2	.271/.340/.480
2019	NYA	MLB	22	533	70	22	2	21	67	50	131	8	4	.262/.337/.450

Breakout: 17%   Improve: 68%   Collapse: 0%   Attrition: 9%   MLB: 74%
Comparables: Addison Russell, Xander Bogaerts, Rougned Odor

With all the talk of Miguel Andujar being snubbed in the Rookie of the Year voting, you'd forget that the Yankees have a rookie with even more promise, and arguably a better 2018 season, in Torres. His wOBA was just 12 points lower than Andujar, and he had just three fewer home runs. Yet the biggest difference was defense, where Torres was a whopping 24 (!!!) runs better by DRS. It's not like it was clutch hitting that made the difference in narrative, either, as Torres also had an edge in WPA by 1.58. In high leverage situations, however little predictability that carries, he had an other-worldly 1.387 OPS. Because Torres coincidentally made the team just after the service time cut-off, the Yankees will have six more years of team control. Another half-decade of well-above-average play at second base is exactly what the doctor ordered for a team that never really found an heir apparent to Robinson Cano.

YEAR	TEAM	LVL	AGE	PA	DRC+	VORP	BABIP	BRR	FRAA	WARP
2016	MYR	A+	19	409	127	26.1	.341	0.2	SS(87): 0.6	1.8
2016	TAM	A+	19	138	118	5.2	.299	-2.9	SS(27): -0.9, 2B(1): 0.0	0.1
2017	TRN	AA	20	139	138	15.5	.295	1.3	SS(19): 2.2, 3B(6): 0.8	1.3
2017	SWB	AAA	20	96	128	7.2	.426	-1.8	SS(9): 1.0, 3B(9): 1.8	0.6
2018	SWB	AAA	21	56	117	4.7	.400	0.1	3B(8): 0.6, 2B(3): 0.0	0.3
2018	NYA	MLB	21	484	121	24.3	.321	0.8	2B(109): 5.4, SS(21): 1.5	3.7
2019	NYA	MLB	22	533	108	25.3	.314	-0.6	2B 3, SS 0	2.7

New York Yankees 2019

Gleyber Torres, continued

Batted Ball Distribution

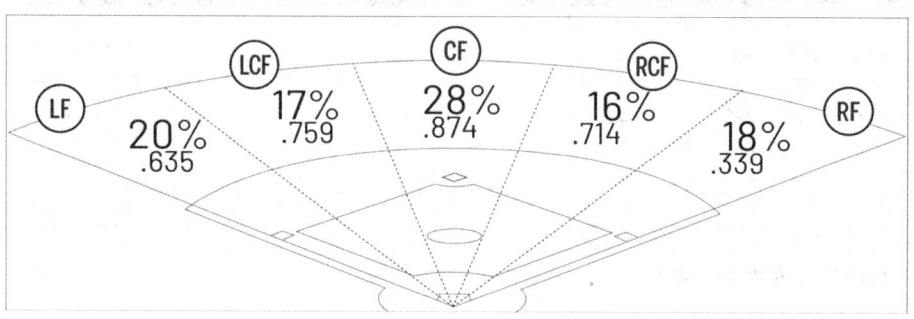

Strike Zone vs LHP   **Strike Zone vs RHP**

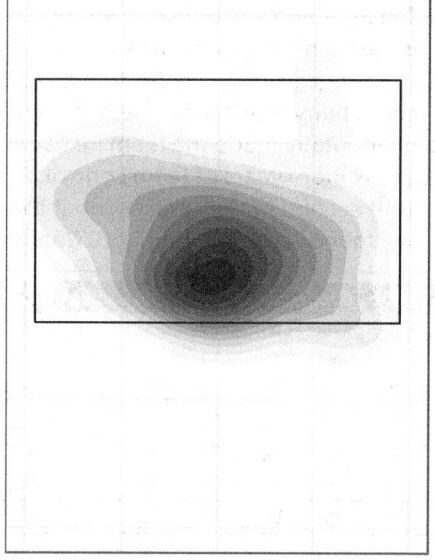

Luke Voit 1B

Born: 02/13/91   Age: 28   Bats: R   Throws: R
Height: 6'3"   Weight: 225   Origin: Round 22, 2013 Draft (#665 overall)

YEAR	TEAM	LVL	AGE	PA	R	2B	3B	HR	RBI	BB	K	SB	CS	AVG/OBP/SLG
2016	SFD	AA	25	546	70	20	5	19	74	52	83	1	2	.297/.372/.477
2017	MEM	AAA	26	307	35	23	1	13	50	29	53	1	1	.327/.407/.565
2017	SLN	MLB	26	124	18	9	0	4	18	7	31	0	0	.246/.306/.430
2018	SLN	MLB	27	13	2	0	0	1	3	2	4	0	0	.182/.308/.455
2018	MEM	AAA	27	271	35	16	2	9	36	31	49	0	1	.299/.391/.500
2018	SWB	AAA	27	32	2	2	0	1	3	3	7	0	0	.310/.375/.483
2018	NYA	MLB	27	148	28	5	0	14	33	15	39	0	0	.333/.405/.689
2019	NYA	MLB	28	459	61	28	1	21	66	39	109	0	0	.280/.350/.506

Breakout: 9%   Improve: 25%   Collapse: 12%   Attrition: 24%   MLB: 64%
Comparables: Nate Freiman, Steve Pearce, Jesus Guzman

If you were ever in the market for baseball paraphernalia centered on Luke Voit, you could head over on to his online shop, where he is selling "LV" shirts in the style of the Louis Vuitton logo. Brian Cashman certainly purchased designer, except it was the equivalent of buying a knock-off and discovering its authenticity after the fact. That being said, Cashman had some clue that he was the real thing, making the decision by the Cardinals to trade him all the more puzzling. He was one of the best hitters in the PCL last season—where the usual park factors caveats apply—and he, despite the small sample size in 2017, had eye-popping exit velocity numbers. He continued both upon arriving in New York, generating barrels at a higher rate than everyone not named Joey Gallo. While regression is a natural conclusion, the Yankees may have finally discovered their first basemen. That'd be Gucci.

YEAR	TEAM	LVL	AGE	PA	DRC+	VORP	BABIP	BRR	FRAA	WARP
2016	SFD	AA	25	546	149	34.1	.323	1.9	1B(104): 2.2, LF(12): 1.1	2.9
2017	MEM	AAA	26	307	163	29.9	.368	-3.6	1B(62): 4.3	2.3
2017	SLN	MLB	26	124	88	0.6	.304	-0.3	1B(31): 1.6	0.2
2018	SLN	MLB	27	13	159	1.4	.167	0.1	1B(3): 0.3	0.2
2018	MEM	AAA	27	271	136	17.0	.345	-1.3	1B(56): 2.1, LF(1): -0.1	1.2
2018	SWB	AAA	27	32	118	1.3	.381	-0.1	1B(3): 0.2	0.1
2018	NYA	MLB	27	148	155	18.4	.380	1.1	1B(32): -2.7	1.1
2019	NYA	MLB	28	459	127	25.1	.332	-1.0	1B 1	2.6

New York Yankees 2019

Luke Voit, continued

Batted Ball Distribution

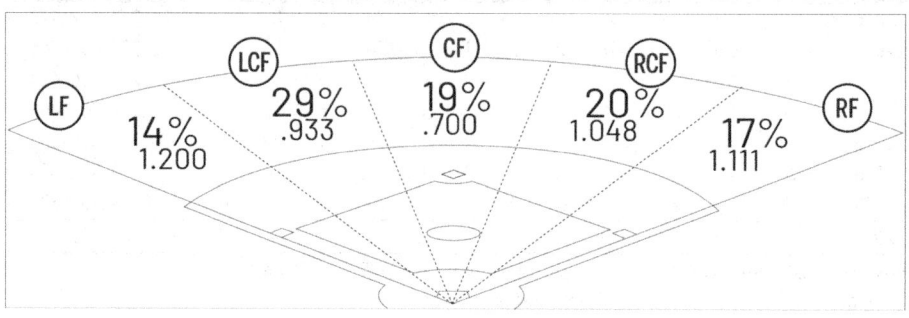

Strike Zone vs LHP   **Strike Zone vs RHP**

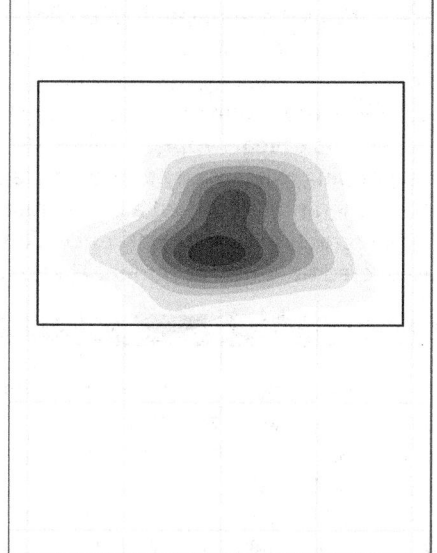

Chance Adams   RHP

Born: 08/10/94   Age: 24   Bats: R   Throws: R
Height: 6'1"   Weight: 220   Origin: Round 5, 2015 Draft (#153 overall)

YEAR	TEAM	LVL	AGE	W	L	SV	G	GS	IP	H	HR	BB/9	K/9	K	GB%	BABIP
2016	TAM	A+	21	5	0	0	12	12	57^2	41	4	2.3	11.4	73	42%	.276
2016	TRN	AA	21	8	1	0	13	12	69^2	35	5	3.1	9.2	71	47%	.181
2017	TRN	AA	22	4	0	0	6	6	35	23	2	3.9	8.2	32	43%	.228
2017	SWB	AAA	22	11	5	0	21	21	115^1	81	9	3.4	8.0	103	42%	.236
2018	SWB	AAA	23	4	5	0	27	23	113	101	16	4.6	9.0	113	42%	.282
2018	NYA	MLB	23	0	1	0	3	1	7^2	8	3	4.7	4.7	4	38%	.217
2019	NYA	MLB	24	3	3	0	30	5	51^2	45	7	4.1	8.4	48	41%	.276

Breakout: 15%   Improve: 27%   Collapse: 33%   Attrition: 38%   MLB: 72%
Comparables: Aaron Blair, Keyvius Sampson, Adam Warren

ABBA said you should *Take a Chance on Me,* but that wasn't so for Chance Adams. Formerly considered a sleeper pitching prospect, he gained some notice after pitching to the tune of a 2.89 ERA at Scranton in 2017. The thinking was that with one injury, Chance would be on his way. That didn't happen until August 4th, when he made his first major league start at Fenway Park. He lost the game, allowing home runs to Mitch Moreland and JD Martinez. That mirrored his minor league season, where his command suffered and his flyball tendencies became home run tendencies. The team has announced he will get an opportunity to make the team as a starter out of Spring Training, so he has just one more Chance at redemption.

YEAR	TEAM	LVL	AGE	WHIP	ERA	DRA	WARP	MPH	FB%	WHF	CSP
2016	TAM	A+	21	0.97	2.65	2.39	2.0				
2016	TRN	AA	21	0.85	2.07	3.15	1.6				
2017	TRN	AA	22	1.09	1.03	3.57	0.7				
2017	SWB	AAA	22	1.08	2.89	4.14	2.0				
2018	SWB	AAA	23	1.41	4.78	4.15	1.8				
2018	NYA	MLB	23	1.57	7.04	7.07	-0.2	94.2	66.7	5.2	41.6
2019	NYA	MLB	24	1.30	4.39	4.52	0.5	94.0	68.7	5.4	42.9

Chance Adams, continued

Pitch Shape vs LHH	Pitch Shape vs RHH
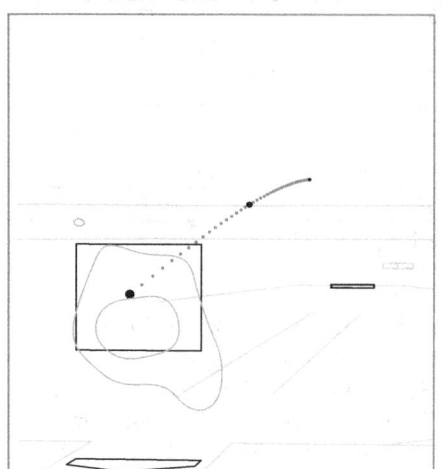	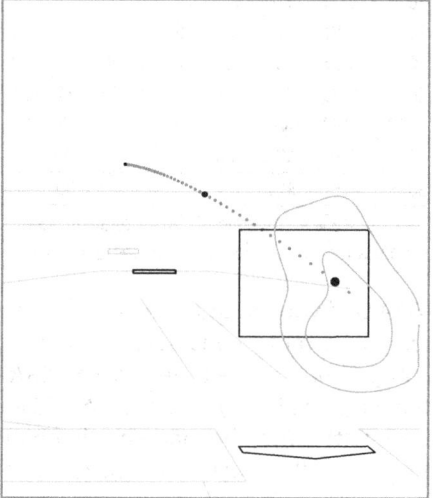

Type	Frequency	Velocity	H Movement	V Movement
● Fastball	66.7%	93 [102]	-2.9 [118]	-15.1 [102]
☐ Sinker				
+ Cutter				
▲ Changeup	0.7%	84.8 [98]	-12 [96]	-22.1 [116]
✕ Splitter				
▽ Slider	13.7%	85.1 [103]	8.2 [115]	-32.6 [101]
◇ Curveball	19.0%	79 [102]	14.8 [129]	-43.6 [110]
⊕ Slow Curveball				
✳ Knuckleball				
▼ Screwball				

Dellin Betances   RHP
Born: 03/23/88   Age: 31   Bats: R   Throws: R
Height: 6'8"   Weight: 265   Origin: Round 8, 2006 Draft (#254 overall)

YEAR	TEAM	LVL	AGE	W	L	SV	G	GS	IP	H	HR	BB/9	K/9	K	GB%	BABIP
2016	NYA	MLB	28	3	6	12	73	0	73	54	5	3.5	15.5	126	56%	.353
2017	NYA	MLB	29	3	6	10	66	0	59^2	29	3	6.6	15.1	100	49%	.252
2018	NYA	MLB	30	4	6	4	66	0	66^2	44	7	3.5	15.5	115	46%	.311
2019	NYA	MLB	31	3	3	5	56	0	58	41	5	4.1	13.2	86	48%	.292

Breakout: 28%   Improve: 35%   Collapse: 40%   Attrition: 17%   MLB: 93%
Comparables: David Robertson, Jonathan Papelbon, B.J. Ryan

Watching Betances is very much like watching a world-class tightrope act. One moment you're swept up by the marvel of it, and the next, you're genuinely concerned that he is going to take a fall. The latter was the case early this season, when he had a 4.50 ERA through May, and his 2017 struggles to find the plate continued. He reclaimed his balance, though, pitching to a phenomenal 1.85 ERA with 75 strikeouts over 43 2/3 innings after June 1st. In totality, his resume is nothing short of impressive: not a single reliever has more innings pitched since 2014, and only one (Wade Davis) has more RA9-WAR. Considering Davis just got $52 million, it's easy to imagine someone (likely another team, if he is still disgruntled with Yankees ownership after a tumultuous arbitration heading in 2017) will be salivating to add his services when he becomes a free agent next season. That's the thing about a tight-rope act: they must be good, or they'd have fallen before the night you saw the show.

YEAR	TEAM	LVL	AGE	WHIP	ERA	DRA	WARP	MPH	FB%	WHF	CSP
2016	NYA	MLB	28	1.12	3.08	1.89	2.6	100.8	43.4	17.1	43.4
2017	NYA	MLB	29	1.22	2.87	3.04	1.4	100.2	46.2	13.3	44.1
2018	NYA	MLB	30	1.05	2.70	2.15	2.1	99.7	47.8	16	47.1
2019	NYA	MLB	31	1.15	2.53	2.83	1.6	99.3	45.8	15.3	44.9

Dellin Betances, continued

Pitch Shape vs LHH

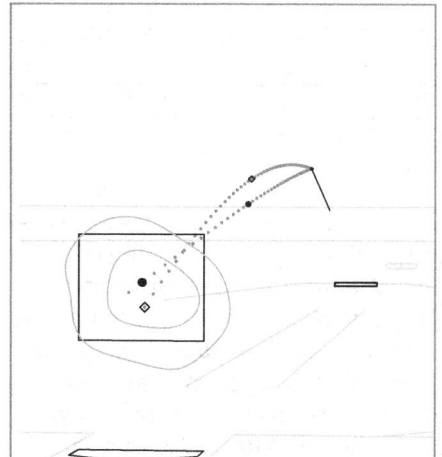

Pitch Shape vs RHH

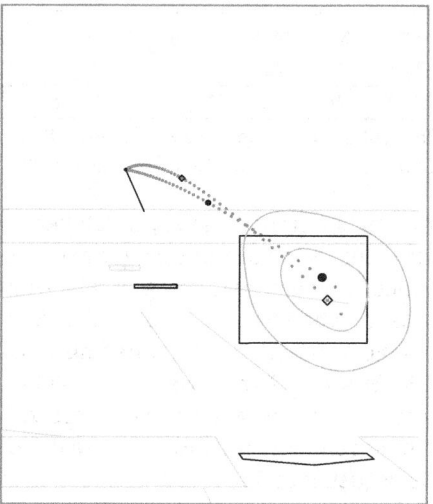

Type	Frequency	Velocity	H Movement	V Movement
● Fastball	47.8%	98.1 [118]	-4.9 [108]	-11.2 [114]
☐ Sinker				
+ Cutter				
▲ Changeup	0.1%	90.1 [119]	-8.2 [116]	-20.9 [119]
✕ Splitter				
▽ Slider				
◇ Curveball	52.1%	85.4 [126]	8.4 [102]	-37.2 [124]
⊕ Slow Curveball				
✳ Knuckleball				
▼ Screwball				

Zack Britton   LHP

Born: 12/22/87   Age: 31   Bats: L   Throws: L
Height: 6'3"   Weight: 195   Origin: Round 3, 2006 Draft (#85 overall)

YEAR	TEAM	LVL	AGE	W	L	SV	G	GS	IP	H	HR	BB/9	K/9	K	GB%	BABIP
2016	BAL	MLB	28	2	1	47	69	0	67	38	1	2.4	9.9	74	80%	.230
2017	BAL	MLB	29	2	1	15	38	0	37^1	39	1	4.3	7.0	29	75%	.336
2018	BAL	MLB	30	1	0	4	16	0	15^2	11	1	5.7	7.5	13	64%	.263
2018	NYA	MLB	30	1	0	3	25	0	25	18	2	4.0	7.6	21	78%	.229
2019	NYA	MLB	31	3	3	4	50	0	53	47	4	4.1	7.9	47	65%	.286

Breakout: 15%   Improve: 37%   Collapse: 30%   Attrition: 13%   MLB: 92%
Comparables: Joe Smith, Mariano Rivera, Francisco Cordero

While Britton is best known for sitting in the bullpen during the 2016 AL Wild Card game, no one would have expected his next playoff appearance would come with the Yankees. Rumors of Manny Machado to the Yankees at the deadline were squashed by sources within the Angelos brain trust, as he would never trade a star to the Bronx. But Britton was fair game, and the O's were able to extract both Dillon Tate and Josh Rogers from their rival, a worthy haul for a rental. Britton lived up to his end of the bargain, but his peripherals are a source of concern. His velocity has taken a dive, and in 2018 his average sinker velocity of 95 mph was the lowest single-season mark since 2013, before he even made the jump to reliever. More worrisome, however, are how hitters are reacting: they've stopped swinging at as many of those pitches out of the zone, providing him fewer of those easy outs and putting him behind in the count more often: his first-strike percentage was a career-low 49.7 percent last season. He can still be serviceable, and any team would be happy to have him, particularly one with a strong framing catcher to reverse some of those worrisome trends. But the days of a 0.54 ERA are long gone.

YEAR	TEAM	LVL	AGE	WHIP	ERA	DRA	WARP	MPH	FB%	WHF	CSP
2016	BAL	MLB	28	0.84	0.54	3.29	1.3	98.6	92.1	18.1	40.6
2017	BAL	MLB	29	1.53	2.89	5.91	-0.3	97.3	94.7	12.4	42.2
2018	BAL	MLB	30	1.34	3.45	7.71	-0.5	96.4	94.4	14.5	42.3
2018	NYA	MLB	30	1.16	2.88	6.55	-0.5	96.6	93.1	12.3	42.8
2019	NYA	MLB	31	1.33	3.78	3.99	0.7	96.6	92.8	14.6	41.7

Zack Britton, continued

Pitch Shape vs LHH

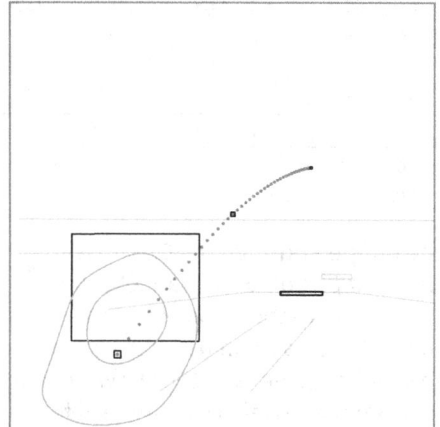

Pitch Shape vs RHH

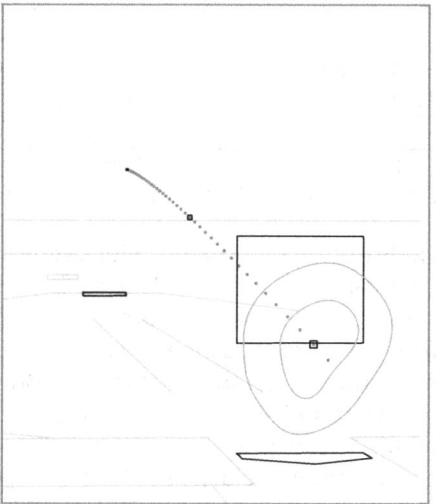

Type	Frequency	Velocity	H Movement	V Movement
● Fastball	1.4%	95.6 [110]	6.1 [103]	-14.1 [105]
□ Sinker	92.2%	95 [113]	9.8 [123]	-21.4 [96]
+ Cutter				
▲ Changeup				
✕ Splitter				
▽ Slider				
◇ Curveball	6.4%	81.5 [111]	-8.8 [104]	-42.5 [112]
⊕ Slow Curveball				
✳ Knuckleball				
▼ Screwball				

Luis Cessa   RHP

Born: 04/25/92   Age: 27   Bats: R   Throws: R
Height: 6'0"   Weight: 210   Origin: International Free Agent, 2008

YEAR	TEAM	LVL	AGE	W	L	SV	G	GS	IP	H	HR	BB/9	K/9	K	GB%	BABIP
2016	SWB	AAA	24	6	3	0	15	14	77[1]	66	8	2.7	8.0	69	47%	.278
2016	NYA	MLB	24	4	4	0	17	9	70[1]	64	16	1.8	5.9	46	45%	.233
2017	SWB	AAA	25	4	6	0	14	13	78[1]	75	7	3.0	7.7	67	48%	.304
2017	NYA	MLB	25	0	3	0	10	5	36	36	7	4.2	7.5	30	46%	.282
2018	TRN	AA	26	0	1	0	2	2	10	6	0	0.9	10.8	12	50%	.250
2018	SWB	AAA	26	3	0	0	6	5	26[1]	19	1	1.4	8.5	25	40%	.250
2018	NYA	MLB	26	1	4	2	16	5	44[2]	51	5	2.6	7.9	39	48%	.333
2019	NYA	MLB	27	4	4	0	35	10	66[2]	67	10	3.3	8.0	59	44%	.295

Breakout: 30%   Improve: 49%   Collapse: 16%   Attrition: 25%   MLB: 81%
Comparables: Brandon Workman, Jacob deGrom, Joe Saunders

Explaining something like replacement level to an average fan sounds impossible; how could you illustrate such a vague archetype? You could start by following and watching Luis Cessa. He checks off most of the boxes: oft-traveled on the Scranton shuttle; a WARP consistently below 1.0; a nebulous mix of starts and relief, both instantly forgotten. Yet the question is always: "Well, then why is Brian Cashman keeping him around?" Partially because of convenience, but also because of peripherals that have made gentle, happy progress. Like the organization as a whole, he is leaning even more on a slider with an ever increasing whiff rate over the course of the season. Still a replacement archetype in the future? Probably. Something more? If he continues his current trend, very possibly.

YEAR	TEAM	LVL	AGE	WHIP	ERA	DRA	WARP	MPH	FB%	WHF	CSP
2016	SWB	AAA	24	1.15	3.03	3.24	1.9				
2016	NYA	MLB	24	1.11	4.35	4.95	0.2	97.5	50.2	11.1	45.8
2017	SWB	AAA	25	1.29	3.45	3.90	1.5				
2017	NYA	MLB	25	1.47	4.75	4.72	0.3	97.8	41.8	11.5	44.5
2018	TRN	AA	26	0.70	2.70	1.59	0.4				
2018	SWB	AAA	26	0.87	2.73	2.86	0.8				
2018	NYA	MLB	26	1.43	5.24	3.23	1.0	96.9	41.6	12.6	45.7
2019	NYA	MLB	27	1.37	4.46	4.58	0.6	96.9	45.2	12	45.9

Luis Cessa, continued

Pitch Shape vs LHH	Pitch Shape vs RHH
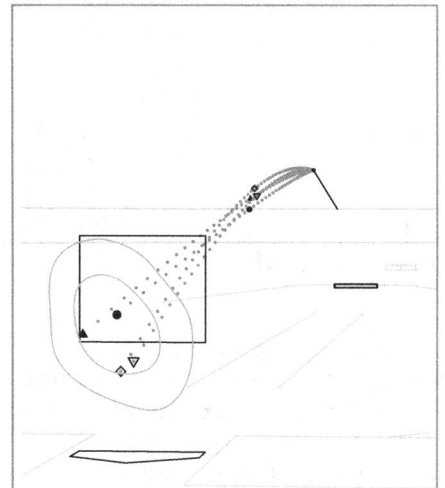	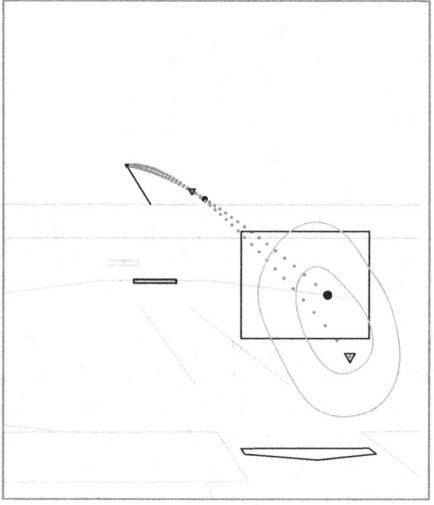

Type	Frequency	Velocity	H Movement	V Movement
● Fastball	41.6%	95 [108]	-6.5 [101]	-14.1 [105]
☐ Sinker				
+ Cutter				
▲ Changeup	12.9%	86.4 [104]	-9.8 [108]	-24.8 [107]
✕ Splitter				
▽ Slider	41.2%	84 [98]	2 [88]	-35.7 [92]
◇ Curveball	4.3%	80.8 [109]	4.5 [86]	-43.9 [109]
✦ Slow Curveball				
✶ Knuckleball				
▼ Screwball				

Aroldis Chapman LHP

Born: 02/28/88 Age: 31 Bats: L Throws: L
Height: 6'4" Weight: 212 Origin: International Free Agent, 2010

YEAR	TEAM	LVL	AGE	W	L	SV	G	GS	IP	H	HR	BB/9	K/9	K	GB%	BABIP
2016	NYA	MLB	28	3	0	20	31	0	31¹	20	2	2.3	12.6	44	38%	.273
2016	CHN	MLB	28	1	1	16	28	0	26²	12	0	3.4	15.5	46	59%	.261
2017	NYA	MLB	29	4	3	22	52	0	50¹	37	3	3.6	12.3	69	48%	.298
2018	NYA	MLB	30	3	0	32	55	0	51¹	24	2	5.3	16.3	93	46%	.268
2019	NYA	MLB	31	3	2	35	50	0	53	38	4	4.1	13.2	78	45%	.296

Breakout: 26%   Improve: 34%   Collapse: 41%   Attrition: 16%   MLB: 93%
Comparables: David Robertson, A.J. Ramos, Jonathan Papelbon

When the Yankees inked Aroldis Chapman to an $86 million deal, the largest ever given to a reliever, the argument against such a move was two-fold: it was a lot of luxury tax space devoted to one good reliever among a cadre of many, and that, frankly, the aging curve for a pitcher like Chapman might not look great. (There was also a third argument.) With the rise of flame-throwing relievers around the league, Chapman would, by this logic, become more pedestrian over time. When he broke into the league in 2010, the average reliever fastball velocity was 92.1 mph. In 2018, it was 93.4 mph. The Yankees' response to this trend was in line with their organizational philosophy, pushing him in the direction of fewer fastballs and more sliders. One positive side effect was his highest strikeout rate since 2014, but the negative one was that he had the highest walk rate (and most wild pitches) to go with it. That last wrinkle needs to be resolved for him to find an aging-curve-resistant form, but it's an encouraging development for a man often considered a one-trick pony.

YEAR	TEAM	LVL	AGE	WHIP	ERA	DRA	WARP	MPH	FB%	WHF	CSP
2016	NYA	MLB	28	0.89	2.01	2.37	0.9	104.1	80.4	19.2	51.3
2016	CHN	MLB	28	0.82	1.01	2.04	0.9	104.2	81.9	20.1	47.5
2017	NYA	MLB	29	1.13	3.22	3.50	0.9	102.4	76.8	15.2	48.5
2018	NYA	MLB	30	1.05	2.45	2.13	1.7	102.3	73.8	16.8	45.8
2019	NYA	MLB	31	1.17	2.39	2.65	1.5	101.9	76.2	16.9	47.3

Aroldis Chapman, continued

Pitch Shape vs LHH

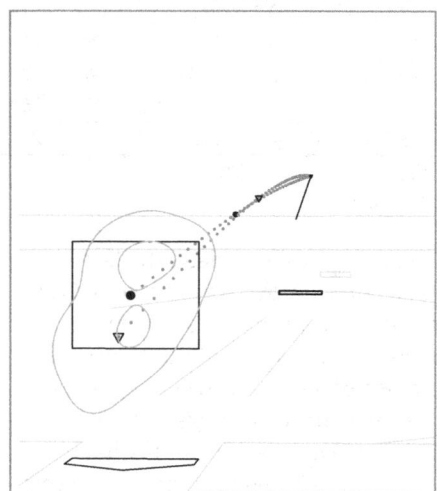

Pitch Shape vs RHH

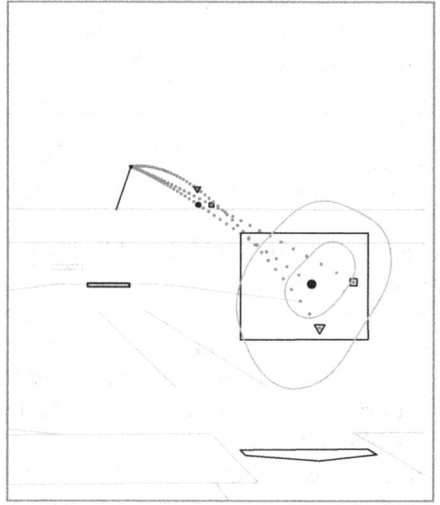

Type	Frequency	Velocity	H Movement	V Movement
● Fastball	68.7%	99.1 [121]	4 [112]	-9.4 [120]
□ Sinker	5.1%	101.5 [145]	12.5 [101]	-10.7 [131]
+ Cutter				
▲ Changeup	0.8%	91.2 [124]	13.7 [87]	-19.5 [123]
× Splitter				
▽ Slider	25.5%	86.5 [109]	-8.9 [118]	-30.6 [107]
◇ Curveball				
✦ Slow Curveball				
✲ Knuckleball				
▼ Screwball				

Domingo German   RHP

Born: 08/04/92   Age: 26   Bats: R   Throws: R
Height: 6'2"   Weight: 175   Origin: International Free Agent, 2009

YEAR	TEAM	LVL	AGE	W	L	SV	G	GS	IP	H	HR	BB/9	K/9	K	GB%	BABIP
2016	CSC	A	23	1	1	0	5	5	26	15	2	0.7	6.2	18	43%	.186
2016	TAM	A+	23	0	2	0	5	5	23^2	26	1	3.4	7.6	20	45%	.342
2017	TRN	AA	24	1	4	0	6	6	33	32	4	2.7	10.4	38	50%	.318
2017	SWB	AAA	24	7	2	0	14	13	76^1	59	5	2.6	9.6	81	46%	.274
2017	NYA	MLB	24	0	1	0	7	0	14^1	11	1	5.7	11.3	18	54%	.294
2018	NYA	MLB	25	2	6	0	21	14	85^2	81	15	3.5	10.7	102	39%	.300
2019	NYA	MLB	26	4	3	0	33	8	58^2	54	8	3.5	9.5	62	41%	.293

Breakout: 21%   Improve: 39%   Collapse: 21%   Attrition: 22%   MLB: 85%
Comparables: James McDonald, Trevor May, Jharel Cotton

Like Jonathan Loaisiga, there are some pitching prospects that sprout up like weeds; so goes the Yankees pitching development machine. German may have been the biggest surprise, though, despite missing most of the season due to an ulnar nerve injury. The results may not have wowed, but the curve did, and people generally pay attention when you have a whiff rate higher than Justin Verlander. The concern is that he relies just on two pitches, not to mention his health; he also underwent Tommy John surgery in 2015. But one can't deny that he might be one of the most talented and overlooked pitchers on the 40-man, with enough talent to fit into, or even lead, an entire rotation. The bell curve of outcomes is wide and likely tends toward worse than better outcomes, but if he were to suddenly become a top-30 pitcher in baseball, not too many keen observers would be surprised.

YEAR	TEAM	LVL	AGE	WHIP	ERA	DRA	WARP	MPH	FB%	WHF	CSP
2016	CSC	A	23	0.65	3.12	3.56	0.5				
2016	TAM	A+	23	1.48	3.04	2.51	0.8				
2017	TRN	AA	24	1.27	3.00	1.88	1.3				
2017	SWB	AAA	24	1.06	2.83	3.54	1.8				
2017	NYA	MLB	24	1.40	3.14	3.15	0.3	98.4	50.4	12.7	40
2018	NYA	MLB	25	1.33	5.57	4.36	0.9	96.3	46.9	15.5	46.9
2019	NYA	MLB	26	1.31	4.09	4.25	0.7	96.2	48.1	15.4	44.6

Domingo German, continued

Pitch Shape vs LHH

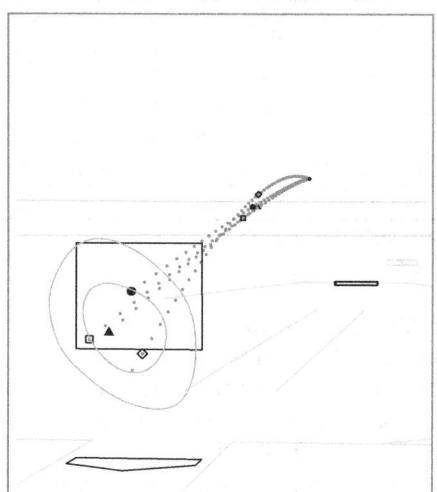

Pitch Shape vs RHH

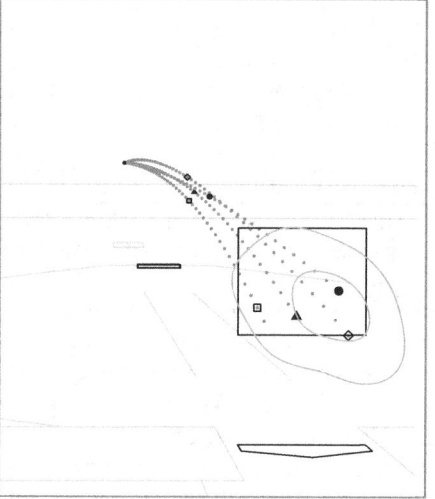

Type	Frequency	Velocity	H Movement	V Movement
● Fastball	29.6%	94.9 [108]	-8 [94]	-13.5 [107]
□ Sinker	17.3%	95.1 [113]	-15 [80]	-20.3 [100]
+ Cutter	0.1%	92.3 [121]	-1.1 [83]	-18.5 [121]
▲ Changeup	17.0%	87.9 [110]	-15.2 [79]	-23.8 [111]
× Splitter				
▽ Slider				
◇ Curveball	36.1%	82.1 [114]	2.8 [79]	-41 [116]
⊕ Slow Curveball				
✳ Knuckleball				
▼ Screwball				

Chad Green   RHP

Born: 05/24/91   Age: 28   Bats: L   Throws: R
Height: 6'3"   Weight: 210   Origin: Round 11, 2013 Draft (#336 overall)

YEAR	TEAM	LVL	AGE	W	L	SV	G	GS	IP	H	HR	BB/9	K/9	K	GB%	BABIP
2016	SWB	AAA	25	7	6	0	16	16	94^2	68	3	2.0	9.5	100	50%	.271
2016	NYA	MLB	25	2	4	1	12	8	45^2	49	12	3.0	10.2	52	44%	.314
2017	SWB	AAA	26	2	1	0	5	5	26^2	32	1	3.7	11.1	33	53%	.397
2017	NYA	MLB	26	5	0	0	40	1	69	34	4	2.2	13.4	103	28%	.236
2018	NYA	MLB	27	8	3	0	63	0	75^2	64	9	1.8	11.2	94	33%	.307
2019	NYA	MLB	28	3	3	0	61	0	64	55	8	3.1	11.1	79	39%	.297

Breakout: 25%   Improve: 49%   Collapse: 16%   Attrition: 13%   MLB: 83%
Comparables: Cory Luebke, Charlie Furbush, Collin McHugh

The only thing that was missing from Chad Green's 2017 season was high leverage opportunities, so it's still remarkable to think he accumulated 2.02 WPA (46th in baseball) working primarily in the sixth and seventh innings. That earned him some eighth inning work, so of course, he regressed all the way down to 1.85 WPA, ranking... 42nd. Green found his rhythm in the second half, allowing just seven earned runs over 29 2/3 innings, maintaining his status as the league's greatest anonymous reliever. Only two relievers have more RA9-WAR over the last two seasons: Blake Treinen and Craig Kimbrel. No one would have expected that from what is, essentially, a one-pitch pitcher; he threw his four-seamer a career high 86% of the time, and that trend likely won't abate.

YEAR	TEAM	LVL	AGE	WHIP	ERA	DRA	WARP	MPH	FB%	WHF	CSP
2016	SWB	AAA	25	0.94	1.52	3.03	2.5				
2016	NYA	MLB	25	1.40	4.73	4.45	0.4	97.1	53	12.9	46.7
2017	SWB	AAA	26	1.61	4.72	3.97	0.5				
2017	NYA	MLB	26	0.74	1.83	2.42	2.1	97.5	69.4	16.4	50.3
2018	NYA	MLB	27	1.04	2.50	3.38	1.3	97.5	86.6	14.9	52.6
2019	NYA	MLB	28	1.19	3.21	3.52	1.2	96.8	74.8	15.1	50.7

Chad Green, continued

Pitch Shape vs LHH   **Pitch Shape vs RHH**

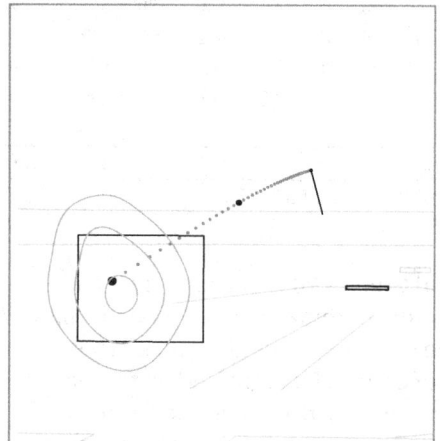 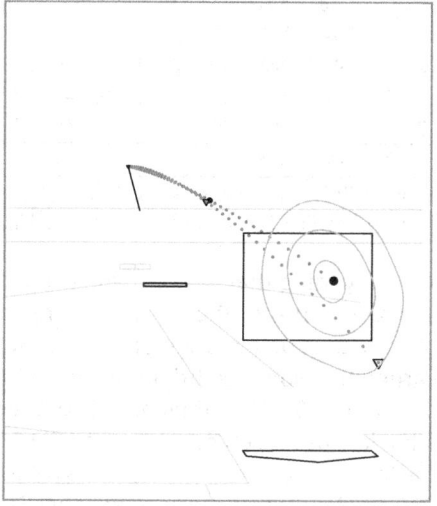

Type	Frequency	Velocity	H Movement	V Movement
● Fastball	86.6%	96.5 [113]	-3.7 [114]	-10.6 [116]
☐ Sinker				
+ Cutter				
▲ Changeup	1.2%	88.3 [112]	-5.7 [130]	-21.6 [117]
✕ Splitter	2.0%	88.3 [115]	-7.8 [101]	-23.9 [124]
▽ Slider	10.2%	87.5 [114]	3.9 [96]	-31.9 [103]
◇ Curveball				
⊕ Slow Curveball				
✳ Knuckleball				
▼ Screwball				

J.A. Happ LHP

Born: 10/19/82   Age: 36   Bats: L   Throws: L
Height: 6'5"   Weight: 205   Origin: Round 3, 2004 Draft (#92 overall)

YEAR	TEAM	LVL	AGE	W	L	SV	G	GS	IP	H	HR	BB/9	K/9	K	GB%	BABIP
2016	TOR	MLB	33	20	4	0	32	32	195	168	22	2.8	7.5	163	44%	.268
2017	TOR	MLB	34	10	11	0	25	25	145^1	145	18	2.8	8.8	142	48%	.302
2018	TOR	MLB	35	10	6	0	20	20	114	99	17	2.8	10.3	130	45%	.285
2018	NYA	MLB	35	7	0	0	11	11	63^2	51	10	2.3	8.9	63	33%	.250
2019	NYA	MLB	36	12	7	0	26	26	156	151	23	3.1	8.6	150	43%	.294

Breakout: 12%   Improve: 40%   Collapse: 21%   Attrition: 12%   MLB: 87%
Comparables: Whitey Ford, Jeff Fassero, Ryan Dempster

The factoid tossed about when the Yankees acquired JA Happ was that he had 2.98 ERA against the Red Sox, so they would both block Boston from getting him themselves and they could use him in a potential playoff spot. Of course, the Yankees did play the Red Sox in the postseason, and… Happ allowed five runs in two innings. Yada yada can't predict baseball yada yada. That doesn't mean it was a poor idea; Happ proved invaluable as a patch for a tattered Yankees rotation into the second half. Even at the age of 36, he has been a consistent three-win pitcher going on a half-decade, the gold standard of third starters. Given the steadiness of his peripherals (even his increased flyball rate was mostly the infield variety), and his remarkable durability, there's little reason to think that he won't reinforce another rotation for a few more years.

YEAR	TEAM	LVL	AGE	WHIP	ERA	DRA	WARP	MPH	FB%	WHF	CSP
2016	TOR	MLB	33	1.17	3.18	4.37	2.2	94.3	73.6	10.4	46.9
2017	TOR	MLB	34	1.31	3.53	4.07	2.4	94.0	71.3	10.5	43.8
2018	TOR	MLB	35	1.18	4.18	3.89	1.9	94.3	74.2	11.7	48
2018	NYA	MLB	35	1.05	2.69	4.00	1.0	94.0	72.3	11.1	48.3
2019	NYA	MLB	36	1.31	4.17	4.33	2.0	92.9	71.4	10.7	45.4

J.A. Happ, continued

Pitch Shape vs LHH

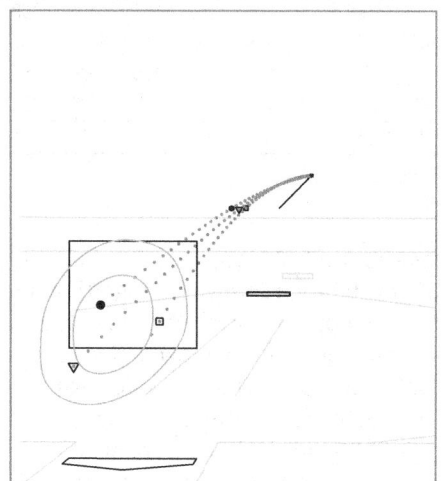

Pitch Shape vs RHH

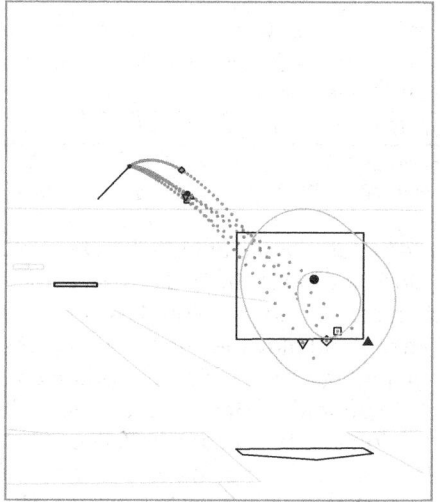

Type	Frequency	Velocity	H Movement	V Movement
● Fastball	59.2%	92.7 [101]	6.6 [100]	-12.9 [109]
☐ Sinker	14.4%	90.8 [92]	12.7 [99]	-21.7 [96]
+ Cutter				
▲ Changeup	12.1%	86.3 [104]	12.7 [92]	-26.1 [104]
✕ Splitter				
▽ Slider	12.7%	85.7 [106]	-2.1 [88]	-28.1 [114]
◇ Curveball	1.7%	76.4 [92]	-1.6 [74]	-47.8 [100]
⊕ Slow Curveball				
✱ Knuckleball				
▼ Screwball				

Jonathan Holder   RHP

Born: 06/09/93   Age: 26   Bats: R   Throws: R
Height: 6'2"   Weight: 235   Origin: Round 6, 2014 Draft (#182 overall)

YEAR	TEAM	LVL	AGE	W	L	SV	G	GS	IP	H	HR	BB/9	K/9	K	GB%	BABIP
2016	TRN	AA	23	3	1	10	28	0	41	27	2	1.5	13.0	59	45%	.298
2016	SWB	AAA	23	2	0	6	12	0	20^1	7	1	0.0	15.5	35	42%	.188
2016	NYA	MLB	23	0	0	0	8	0	8^1	8	1	4.3	5.4	5	37%	.269
2017	SWB	AAA	24	0	0	1	12	0	16	15	1	4.5	11.8	21	40%	.359
2017	NYA	MLB	24	1	1	0	37	0	39^1	45	5	1.8	9.2	40	42%	.348
2018	SWB	AAA	25	1	0	0	4	1	6	5	1	1.5	12.0	8	53%	.286
2018	NYA	MLB	25	1	3	0	60	1	66	53	4	2.6	8.2	60	31%	.261
2019	NYA	MLB	26	2	3	0	50	0	53	51	9	3.5	9.1	54	38%	.290

Breakout: 29%   Improve: 50%   Collapse: 21%   Attrition: 17%   MLB: 85%
Comparables: Jonathan Papelbon, Cory Wade, Daniel Herrera

Another day, another solid reliever created out of thin air in Holder. While every other pitcher in the staff is zigging by backing off their fastball, Holder is one of the few pitchers on the staff who has zagged, throwing his fastball 55 percent of the time, up from about a third of the time a season before. It may have shown up in the results in his 73 ERA-, but it's possible he may adjust and lean more heavily on his new slider in 2019: he saw a decline in his strikeout rate, an increase in his walk rate, and no significant change in his whiff rate or quality of contact. His fastball has zip and is still a plus pitch, but he may benefit from a more backwards approach if he negatively regresses.

YEAR	TEAM	LVL	AGE	WHIP	ERA	DRA	WARP	MPH	FB%	WHF	CSP
2016	TRN	AA	23	0.83	2.20	1.73	1.5				
2016	SWB	AAA	23	0.34	0.89	1.66	0.8				
2016	NYA	MLB	23	1.44	5.40	4.34	0.1	94.7	43.1	12.5	45.9
2017	SWB	AAA	24	1.44	1.69	2.49	0.5				
2017	NYA	MLB	24	1.35	3.89	3.11	0.9	93.5	37.2	13.2	47.9
2018	SWB	AAA	25	1.00	3.00	2.59	0.2				
2018	NYA	MLB	25	1.09	3.14	4.33	0.5	94.2	55.4	11.5	47.5
2019	NYA	MLB	26	1.35	4.67	4.71	0.3	93.6	49.8	12.3	48.1

Jonathan Holder, continued

Pitch Shape vs LHH
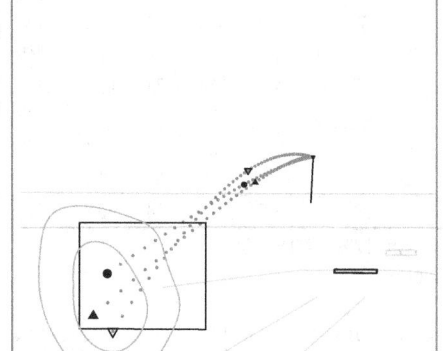

Pitch Shape vs RHH
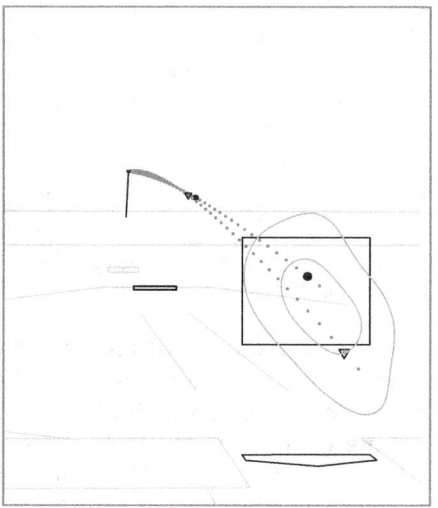

Type	Frequency	Velocity	H Movement	V Movement
● Fastball	55.4%	93 [101]	-1.9 [122]	-14 [106]
☐ Sinker				
+ Cutter	2.2%	87.1 [90]	7.1 [130]	-28.8 [80]
▲ Changeup	16.5%	85.7 [101]	-12.9 [91]	-27.9 [98]
✕ Splitter				
▽ Slider	24.0%	82.7 [92]	8.2 [115]	-37.6 [86]
◇ Curveball	1.9%	76.7 [93]	11.5 [115]	-55.3 [84]
✣ Slow Curveball				
✳ Knuckleball				
▼ Screwball				

Tommy Kahnle   RHP
Born: 08/07/89   Age: 29   Bats: R   Throws: R
Height: 6'1"   Weight: 235   Origin: Round 5, 2010 Draft (#175 overall)

YEAR	TEAM	LVL	AGE	W	L	SV	G	GS	IP	H	HR	BB/9	K/9	K	GB%	BABIP
2016	CHR	AAA	26	1	1	7	23	0	27	17	0	4.0	12.0	36	48%	.283
2016	CHA	MLB	26	0	1	1	29	0	27^1	21	2	6.6	8.2	25	50%	.264
2017	CHA	MLB	27	1	3	0	37	0	36	28	3	1.8	15.0	60	43%	.352
2017	NYA	MLB	27	1	1	0	32	0	26^2	25	1	3.4	12.1	36	40%	.364
2018	SWB	AAA	28	2	2	1	25	0	24^2	23	2	4.0	13.5	37	40%	.375
2018	NYA	MLB	28	2	0	1	24	0	23^1	23	3	5.8	11.6	30	39%	.339
2019	NYA	MLB	29	2	2	0	40	0	42^2	37	5	4.5	10.4	50	42%	.294

Breakout: 17%   Improve: 49%   Collapse: 28%   Attrition: 14%   MLB: 95%
Comparables: Steve Cishek, Al Alburquerque, Jose Valverde

The Yankees didn't give up Blake Rutherford and Ian Clarkin just because they were getting David Robertson and Todd Frazier. No, the hidden prize of that deal was Tommy Kahnle, who had a 165 ERA+ in a White Sox uniform and four and a half years of team control left. Now he's more of an afterthought, and his 2018 was an unmitigated disaster. He was plagued by injury and played just half the season, saw a 2.5 mph drop in velocity, and his command went completely out the window, as he walked 15 batters in just 23 1/3 innings. He was so unspectacular that he was left off the playoff roster entirely. 2019 will be a reset year, but make no mistake: if those negative trends don't reverse course, then one can likely close the book on that trade return's value. Sadly, in a league where starters are working harder and shorter, and relievers are overflowing the bullpen, Kahnle is the example of the risk involved: Relievers are still volatile and fragile creatures.

YEAR	TEAM	LVL	AGE	WHIP	ERA	DRA	WARP	MPH	FB%	WHF	CSP
2016	CHR	AAA	26	1.07	3.00	3.19	0.5				
2016	CHA	MLB	26	1.50	2.63	5.95	-0.3	99.3	73.6	11.5	49.8
2017	CHA	MLB	27	0.97	2.50	2.10	1.2	99.7	72.6	18.2	51.3
2017	NYA	MLB	27	1.31	2.70	2.05	0.9	99.3	58.9	17.2	46.6
2018	SWB	AAA	28	1.38	4.01	1.64	1.0				
2018	NYA	MLB	28	1.63	6.56	4.03	0.2	97.0	54.3	15.2	46
2019	NYA	MLB	29	1.36	3.83	4.05	0.5	98.1	64	15.8	48

Tommy Kahnle, continued

Pitch Shape vs LHH

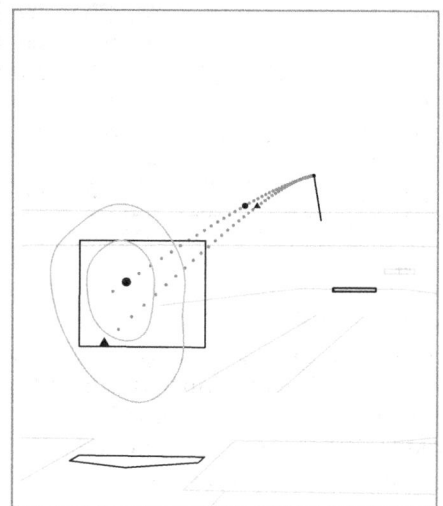

Pitch Shape vs RHH

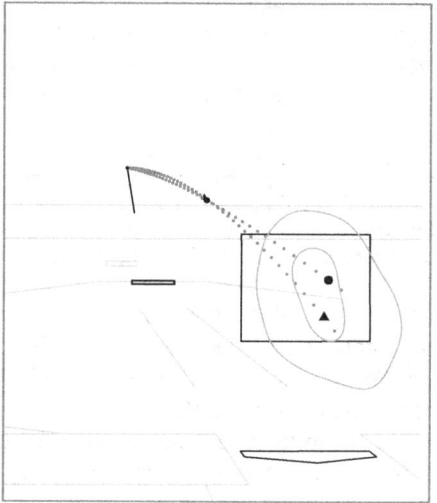

Type	Frequency	Velocity	H Movement	V Movement
● Fastball	54.3%	95.5 [109]	-3.1 [116]	-12 [112]
☐ Sinker				
+ Cutter				
▲ Changeup	40.3%	88.8 [114]	-11.6 [98]	-24.6 [108]
✕ Splitter				
▽ Slider	5.3%	83.5 [96]	7.6 [112]	-34.1 [97]
◇ Curveball				
⊕ Slow Curveball				
✳ Knuckleball				
▼ Screwball				

Jonathan Loaisiga   RHP
Born: 11/02/94   Age: 24   Bats: R   Throws: R
Height: 5'11"   Weight: 165   Origin: International Free Agent, 2012

YEAR	TEAM	LVL	AGE	W	L	SV	G	GS	IP	H	HR	BB/9	K/9	K	GB%	BABIP
2017	YAN	RK	22	0	1	0	6	6	13^2	10	1	1.3	9.9	15	58%	.257
2017	STA	A-	22	1	0	0	4	4	17	7	0	0.5	9.5	18	51%	.171
2018	TAM	A+	23	3	0	0	4	4	20	19	0	0.4	11.7	26	54%	.365
2018	TRN	AA	23	3	1	0	9	9	34^1	37	6	1.6	10.5	40	39%	.356
2018	NYA	MLB	23	2	0	0	9	4	24^2	26	3	4.4	12.0	33	52%	.383
2019	NYA	MLB	24	4	3	0	10	10	50	51	9	3.5	8.8	49	42%	.299

Breakout: 27%   Improve: 47%   Collapse: 13%   Attrition: 25%   MLB: 75%
Comparables: David Paulino, Daniel Norris, Gio Gonzalez

They say that lasagna tastes the best the day after cooking, so it makes sense that Jonathan Loaisiga (with nom de guerre, "Johnny Lasagna") looks better start after start. And sure, there were only five major league starts to speak of, but the small sample raised a ton of eyebrows. His fastball not only touches the mid-to-high 90s, but it also has a phenomenal spin rate of 2,341 rpm. Meanwhile, his slider had a whopping 42% whiff rate, and his change could be deadly against left-handers. All of the ingredients are there for a fully fledged starting pitcher—or, ho-hum, just another high leverage reliever. The front office has bounced him around Trenton and Scranton, but you would imagine that in 2019 and beyond, he will get more trial runs at success. If he adds command to his existing repertoire, they will have manufactured a middle of the rotation starter out of whole cloth.

YEAR	TEAM	LVL	AGE	WHIP	ERA	DRA	WARP	MPH	FB%	WHF	CSP
2017	YAN	RK	22	0.88	2.63	2.59	0.5				
2017	STA	A-	22	0.47	0.53	2.82	0.5				
2018	TAM	A+	23	1.00	1.35	3.60	0.4				
2018	TRN	AA	23	1.25	3.93	3.08	0.9				
2018	NYA	MLB	23	1.54	5.11	3.29	0.5	97.5	55.7	14.8	46.1
2019	NYA	MLB	24	1.45	4.66	4.85	0.3	97.3	57.4	15.3	47.5

Jonathan Loaisiga, continued

Pitch Shape vs LHH

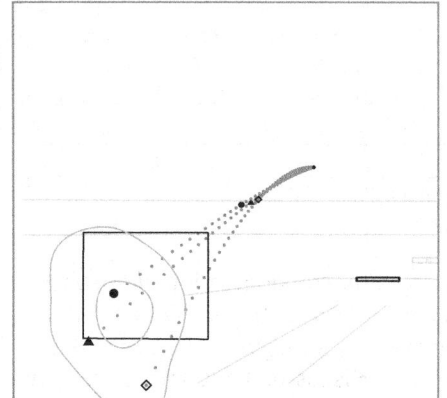

Pitch Shape vs RHH

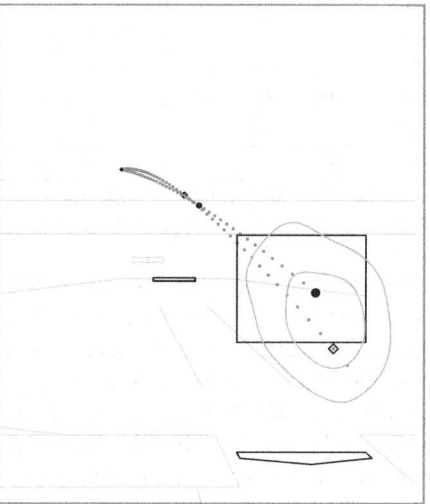

Type	Frequency	Velocity	H Movement	V Movement
● Fastball	55.7%	96.1 [111]	-4.4 [111]	-12 [112]
☐ Sinker				
+ Cutter				
▲ Changeup	13.2%	88.2 [112]	-10.9 [102]	-23 [113]
✕ Splitter				
▽ Slider				
◇ Curveball	31.1%	84.7 [123]	5.1 [89]	-36.1 [127]
⊕ Slow Curveball				
✶ Knuckleball				
▼ Screwball				

Adam Ottavino RHP

Born: 11/22/85   Age: 33   Bats: B   Throws: R
Height: 6'5"   Weight: 220   Origin: Round 1, 2006 Draft (#30 overall)

YEAR	TEAM	LVL	AGE	W	L	SV	G	GS	IP	H	HR	BB/9	K/9	K	GB%	BABIP
2016	COL	MLB	30	1	3	7	34	0	27	18	3	2.3	11.7	35	62%	.250
2017	COL	MLB	31	2	3	0	63	0	53¹	48	8	6.6	10.6	63	40%	.310
2018	COL	MLB	32	6	4	6	75	0	77²	41	5	4.2	13.0	112	44%	.242
2019	NYA	MLB	33	3	3	0	56	0	58	47	7	4.5	11.0	72	45%	.288

Breakout: 22%   Improve: 45%   Collapse: 31%   Attrition: 8%   MLB: 93%
Comparables: Pedro Strop, Damaso Marte, Brian Fuentes

In a land of flat pitches, Ottavino's slider swept just about harder'n anybody else's slider last year. A diabolical delivery masked that filthy breaker, and it didn't help hitters that he sits 94 with a couple ticks on top from the extension and deception. He's older than you think he is, mostly because it took him a long time to stay healthy enough and find opportunity to dominate again. He's never really had a shot at sea-level home cooking. Then again, outside of a really poor two weeks in 2017, he hasn't ever really struggled to throw disgusting inning after disgusting inning at a mile high, either. Payment is due his way in free agency, and due it shall inevitably come. We've seen more than enough at this point to know that he'll be very, very good...if he's healthy.

YEAR	TEAM	LVL	AGE	WHIP	ERA	DRA	WARP	MPH	FB%	WHF	CSP
2016	COL	MLB	30	0.93	2.67	4.22	0.2	96.3	52.6	12.8	44.8
2017	COL	MLB	31	1.63	5.06	6.10	-0.6	96.3	50.2	9.9	46.3
2018	COL	MLB	32	0.99	2.43	3.02	1.7	95.7	43.1	13	47.9
2019	NYA	MLB	33	1.30	3.67	3.92	0.8	94.9	46.2	11.7	46.1

Adam Ottavino, continued

Pitch Shape vs LHH

Pitch Shape vs RHH

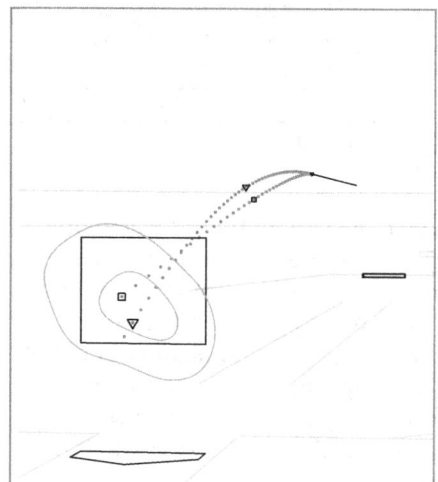
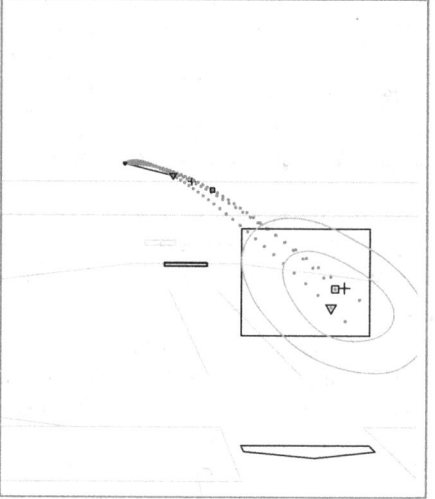

Type	Frequency	Velocity	H Movement	V Movement
● Fastball	4.6%	94.3 [106]	-8.3 [92]	-18.4 [92]
□ Sinker	38.6%	94.5 [110]	-11.6 [108]	-21.1 [98]
+ Cutter	10.1%	87.5 [92]	6 [124]	-25.4 [93]
▲ Changeup	0.4%	89.8 [118]	-7.6 [120]	-26.8 [102]
× Splitter				
▽ Slider	46.3%	82 [89]	14.9 [143]	-35.8 [92]
◇ Curveball				
✥ Slow Curveball				
✳ Knuckleball				
▼ Screwball				

James Paxton   LHP

Born: 11/06/88   Age: 30   Bats: L   Throws: L
Height: 6'4"   Weight: 235   Origin: Round 4, 2010 Draft (#132 overall)

YEAR	TEAM	LVL	AGE	W	L	SV	G	GS	IP	H	HR	BB/9	K/9	K	GB%	BABIP
2016	TAC	AAA	27	4	3	0	11	11	50^2	43	6	2.7	9.4	53	52%	.285
2016	SEA	MLB	27	6	7	0	20	20	121	134	9	1.8	8.7	117	49%	.347
2017	SEA	MLB	28	12	5	0	24	24	136	113	9	2.4	10.3	156	46%	.300
2018	SEA	MLB	29	11	6	0	28	28	160^1	134	23	2.4	11.7	208	41%	.299
2019	NYA	MLB	30	12	6	0	26	26	156	138	19	2.9	10.6	184	44%	.302

Breakout: 15%   Improve: 52%   Collapse: 20%   Attrition: 6%   MLB: 96%
Comparables: Carlos Carrasco, Felix Hernandez, Jacob deGrom

Let's talk for a moment about curses. It takes a special kind of talent to both throw a no-hitter and, in a separate start, strikeout 16 A's over 7 innings. To do that, and set a career high in innings and strike outs and STILL leave the season feeling somehow unfulfilled requires a special level of talent, and that's what Paxton is. Since the moment in 2016 when he dropped his arm slot and tacked 4-5 mph on his fastball, he has been one of the most gifted, sporadically-dominant pitchers on the planet. The levels of achievement possible for a 200-inning Paxton season are nearly as great as any in the game. That he can be just what he is—an incredible number two starter and the greatest left-hander Seattle has had since Randy Johnson - and still leave us expecting more is a testament to his ability. Oh yeah, and a curse.

YEAR	TEAM	LVL	AGE	WHIP	ERA	DRA	WARP	MPH	FB%	WHF	CSP
2016	TAC	AAA	27	1.14	3.73	3.17	1.3				
2016	SEA	MLB	27	1.31	3.79	3.73	2.3	99.7	62.4	12.8	50.4
2017	SEA	MLB	28	1.10	2.98	2.63	4.5	97.6	65.6	13.5	49.5
2018	SEA	MLB	29	1.10	3.76	2.67	4.9	97.5	63.7	15.8	53
2019	NYA	MLB	30	1.21	3.32	3.43	3.6	97.2	63.8	14.4	51

James Paxton, continued

	Pitch Shape vs LHH	Pitch Shape vs RHH
	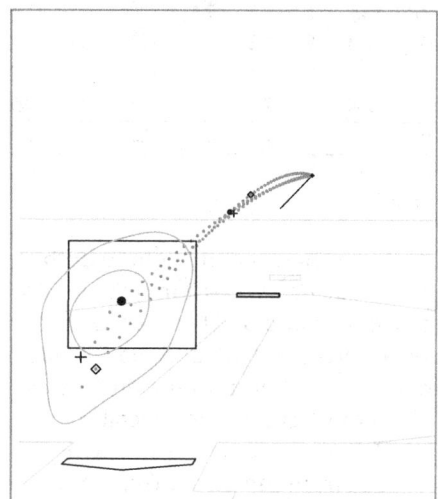	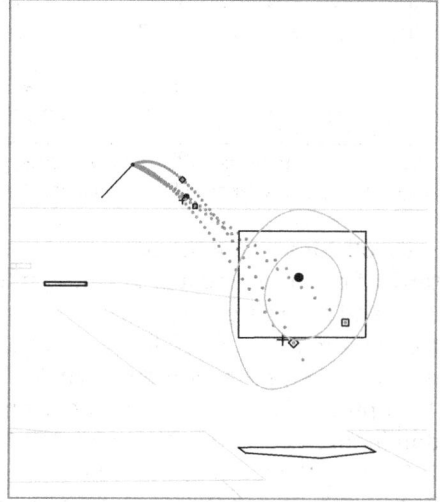

Type	Frequency	Velocity	H Movement	V Movement
● Fastball	55.7%	95.9 [111]	10.3 [83]	-12.7 [110]
☐ Sinker	8.0%	95.5 [115]	14.5 [84]	-16.3 [113]
+ Cutter	14.4%	89.5 [104]	0.4 [86]	-26.1 [91]
▲ Changeup	0.4%	86.5 [105]	11.3 [100]	-24.9 [107]
✕ Splitter				
▽ Slider				
◇ Curveball	21.5%	81.6 [112]	-2.8 [79]	-43.8 [110]
⊕ Slow Curveball				
✻ Knuckleball				
▼ Screwball				

CC Sabathia LHP

Born: 07/21/80   Age: 38   Bats: L   Throws: L
Height: 6'6"   Weight: 300   Origin: Round 1, 1998 Draft (#20 overall)

YEAR	TEAM	LVL	AGE	W	L	SV	G	GS	IP	H	HR	BB/9	K/9	K	GB%	BABIP
2016	NYA	MLB	35	9	12	0	30	30	179^2	172	22	3.3	7.6	152	52%	.288
2017	NYA	MLB	36	14	5	0	27	27	148^2	139	21	3.0	7.3	120	51%	.276
2018	NYA	MLB	37	9	7	0	29	29	153	150	19	3.0	8.2	140	45%	.295
2019	NYA	MLB	38	9	6	0	21	21	119^2	126	19	3.4	7.4	99	47%	.298

Breakout: 17%   Improve: 37%   Collapse: 16%   Attrition: 6%   MLB: 75%
Comparables: John Lackey, Derek Lowe, Andy Pettitte

Sabathia's 2018 season can be summed up by four words: "That's for you, [redacted]." With just two innings to go before reaching a $500,000 incentive for throwing 155 innings, he instead opted to plunk Jesus Sucre in retaliation for the Rays throwing at Austin Romine's head, leading to an ejection in his final start. It was a fiery moment, and it's how he will likely be remembered in pinstripes, putting his teammates above himself and remaining fiercely loyal and defensive for them. That isn't even to mention his performance. He now has a 117 ERA+ over his last three seasons, a marked turnaround from his 2013-2015 nadir. Overall, he had an illustrious Yankees career that will be nothing but fondly remembered: a 3.75 ERA over 1810 2/3 innings, three top-five Cy Young finishes, a World Series championship, and postseason performances in 2009, 2012, and 2017 that will be reminisced on for time immemorial. That's for you, New York.

YEAR	TEAM	LVL	AGE	WHIP	ERA	DRA	WARP	MPH	FB%	WHF	CSP
2016	NYA	MLB	35	1.32	3.91	4.52	1.7	93.4	63.6	10.6	44
2017	NYA	MLB	36	1.27	3.69	3.92	2.7	92.9	53.2	9.6	45.3
2018	NYA	MLB	37	1.31	3.65	4.40	1.6	91.8	59	11.8	45.7
2019	NYA	MLB	38	1.43	4.67	4.85	0.8	91.1	57	10.5	43.9

CC Sabathia, continued

Pitch Shape vs LHH

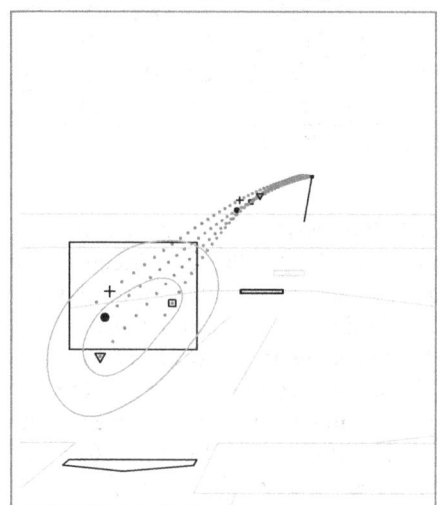

Pitch Shape vs RHH

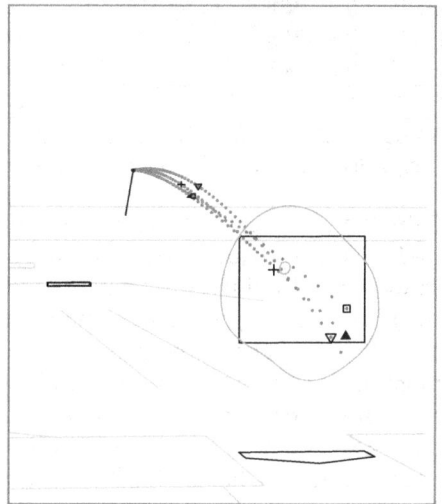

Type	Frequency	Velocity	H Movement	V Movement
● Fastball	2.0%	91.6 [97]	3 [117]	-17.4 [95]
□ Sinker	14.8%	90.5 [90]	12.6 [100]	-22.5 [93]
+ Cutter	42.3%	89.4 [103]	-0.9 [94]	-21.2 [110]
▲ Changeup	10.1%	83.8 [94]	8.7 [114]	-28.1 [98]
× Splitter				
▽ Slider	30.8%	80.3 [82]	-9.8 [121]	-37 [88]
◇ Curveball				
⊕ Slow Curveball				
✳ Knuckleball				
▼ Screwball				

Luis Severino   RHP

Born: 02/20/94   Age: 25   Bats: R   Throws: R
Height: 6'2"   Weight: 215   Origin: International Free Agent, 2011

YEAR	TEAM	LVL	AGE	W	L	SV	G	GS	IP	H	HR	BB/9	K/9	K	GB%	BABIP
2016	SWB	AAA	22	8	1	0	13	12	77¹	75	4	2.1	9.1	78	46%	.321
2016	NYA	MLB	22	3	8	0	22	11	71	78	11	3.2	8.4	66	45%	.324
2017	NYA	MLB	23	14	6	0	31	31	193¹	150	21	2.4	10.7	230	50%	.272
2018	NYA	MLB	24	19	8	0	32	32	191¹	173	19	2.2	10.3	220	42%	.314
2019	NYA	MLB	25	11	6	0	24	24	144	129	19	2.8	9.9	159	44%	.294

Breakout: 24%   Improve: 57%   Collapse: 17%   Attrition: 11%   MLB: 98%
Comparables: Gerrit Cole, Aaron Nola, Tommy Hanson

One of the big question marks going into 2019 will be the Yankees' rotation, but up until a few months ago, people wouldn't have expected Luis Severino to be part of the problem. The postseason may have left a lasting impression because of his six earned runs in seven innings, though it could have been the result of tipping pitches. The bigger issue was his slider, though, which while nearly unhittable in the first half, lost about 150 RPM of spin from April to August. It featured less vertical drop and break. Barring any new information, this will likely confound analysts until he either figures it out or it becomes the new normal. Was the issue mechanics? Was it just fatigue? Whatever the reason, the Yankees will need first half Severino instead of the second half variety if they hope to patch together a competent rotation.

YEAR	TEAM	LVL	AGE	WHIP	ERA	DRA	WARP	MPH	FB%	WHF	CSP
2016	SWB	AAA	22	1.20	3.49	3.14	1.9				
2016	NYA	MLB	22	1.45	5.83	5.23	0.0	99.0	56	9.9	47.5
2017	NYA	MLB	23	1.04	2.98	2.68	6.2	99.5	51.4	13.7	49.4
2018	NYA	MLB	24	1.14	3.39	2.79	5.6	99.4	50.5	13.3	51.2
2019	NYA	MLB	25	1.20	3.55	3.67	2.9	99.1	52.7	13.4	50.9

Luis Severino, continued

Pitch Shape vs LHH

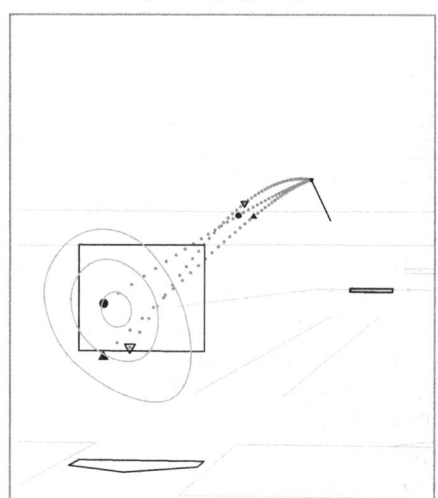

Pitch Shape vs RHH

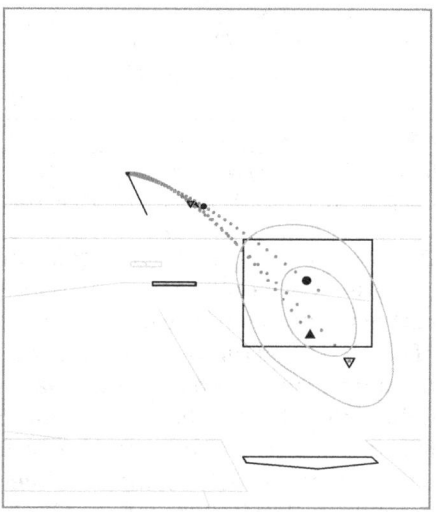

Type	Frequency	Velocity	H Movement	V Movement
● Fastball	50.5%	97.9 [117]	-5.3 [107]	-11.2 [114]
☐ Sinker				
+ Cutter	0.1%	92.5 [122]	4.7 [117]	-21.6 [109]
▲ Changeup	13.6%	88.4 [112]	-10.1 [106]	-22.1 [116]
✕ Splitter				
▽ Slider	35.9%	88.4 [117]	9.2 [119]	-33.4 [99]
◇ Curveball				
⊕ Slow Curveball				
✳ Knuckleball				
▼ Screwball				

Masahiro Tanaka   RHP

Born: 11/01/88   Age: 30   Bats: R   Throws: R
Height: 6'3"   Weight: 215   Origin: International Free Agent, 2014

YEAR	TEAM	LVL	AGE	W	L	SV	G	GS	IP	H	HR	BB/9	K/9	K	GB%	BABIP
2016	NYA	MLB	27	14	4	0	31	31	199^2	179	22	1.6	7.4	165	49%	.271
2017	NYA	MLB	28	13	12	0	30	30	178^1	180	35	2.1	9.8	194	50%	.306
2018	NYA	MLB	29	12	6	0	27	27	156	141	25	2.0	9.2	159	49%	.284
2019	NYA	MLB	30	12	7	0	27	27	162	152	22	2.4	8.3	150	48%	.289

Breakout: 10%   Improve: 50%   Collapse: 15%   Attrition: 2%   MLB: 96%
Comparables: Jim Bunning, Billy Pierce, Aaron Harang

When Masahiro Tanaka came over from NPB, a variety of his skills were seen as transferable to the big leagues: command, a deadly splitter, and the ability to pitch in high drama, cultivated from Koshien to sealing the deal in Game Six and Seven of the 2013 Japan Series. His Achilles heel was, and still is in 2018, his fastball and sinker. Those pitches had respective .594 and .560 opposing slugging percentages in 2018, but Larry Rothschild and the Yankees found a solution: stop throwing them. He had the second-lowest fastball percentage in baseball (only to CC Sabathia) and he rode it to a stellar second half (2.98 FIP). He followed up with a phenomenal October, putting his career postseason ERA at 1.80 in 30 innings. His PRP-injected elbow will always be a specter, but the organization is happy that they get two more years of Ma-kun.

YEAR	TEAM	LVL	AGE	WHIP	ERA	DRA	WARP	MPH	FB%	WHF	CSP
2016	NYA	MLB	27	1.08	3.07	3.26	4.8	93.6	45	11.7	46.6
2017	NYA	MLB	28	1.24	4.74	3.91	3.3	94.0	37.6	15.8	41.7
2018	NYA	MLB	29	1.13	3.75	3.95	2.5	93.6	31.5	14.8	44
2019	NYA	MLB	30	1.20	3.88	4.02	2.6	93.0	37.3	14.3	43.7

Masahiro Tanaka, continued

Pitch Shape vs LHH

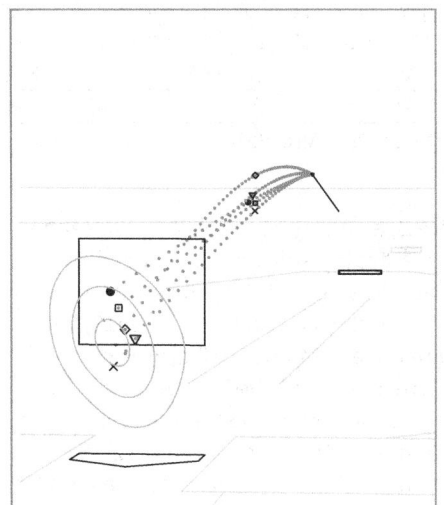

Pitch Shape vs RHH

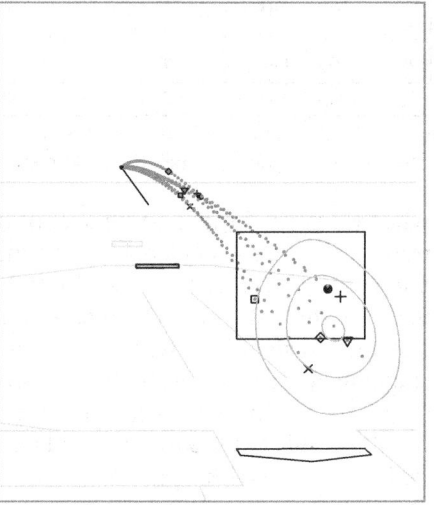

Type	Frequency	Velocity	H Movement	V Movement
● Fastball	21.3%	92.2 [99]	-7.5 [96]	-14.1 [105]
☐ Sinker	4.7%	91.1 [93]	-13.4 [94]	-21.1 [97]
+ Cutter	5.4%	89.4 [104]	-1.9 [78]	-19.3 [118]
▲ Changeup				
✕ Splitter	31.2%	87.2 [108]	-8.9 [97]	-29.3 [101]
▽ Slider	33.5%	83.7 [97]	6.3 [106]	-34 [97]
◇ Curveball	3.9%	77.2 [96]	6.9 [96]	-48 [100]
⊕ Slow Curveball				
✳ Knuckleball				
▼ Screwball				

Jacoby Ellsbury CF
Born: 09/11/83 Age: 35 Bats: L Throws: L
Height: 6'1" Weight: 195 Origin: Round 1, 2005 Draft (#23 overall)

YEAR	TEAM	LVL	AGE	PA	R	2B	3B	HR	RBI	BB	K	SB	CS	AVG/OBP/SLG
2016	NYA	MLB	32	626	71	24	5	9	56	54	84	20	8	.263/.330/.374
2017	NYA	MLB	33	409	65	20	4	7	39	41	63	22	3	.264/.348/.402
2019	NYA	MLB	35	73	9	3	1	1	7	7	11	3	1	.262/.342/.385

Breakout: 0%   Improve: 12%   Collapse: 25%   Attrition: 26%   MLB: 79%
Comparables: Mike Kingery, Lloyd Waner, Brady Clark

On August 29th, it was announced that Yankee Stadium would soon feature a wine bar sporting a "cask-based aesthetic." One can only assume that it is of the Amontillado variety, and their unfortunate friend to live behind the cask is none other than Jacoby Ellsbury. The former All-Star might as well live in a wall behind the bar; he failed to appear in a single game due to a right oblique strain, which led to a left hip issue, and then plantar fasciitis, which then snowballed into a torn labrum in that same hip. With two years still remaining on his bloated deal, but the team skating under the luxury tax threshold, the front office is likely to reinvest the insurance money in more personnel... and a bigger bar.

YEAR	TEAM	LVL	AGE	PA	DRC+	VORP	BABIP	BRR	FRAA	WARP
2016	NYA	MLB	32	626	93	12.3	.295	2.3	CF(148): -14.5	0.3
2017	NYA	MLB	33	409	97	16.4	.304	1.4	CF(97): -5.8	0.8
2019	NYA	MLB	35	73	97	2.9	.303	0.3	CF -1	0.1

Estevan Florial CF
Born: 11/25/97 Age: 21 Bats: L Throws: R
Height: 6'1" Weight: 185 Origin: International Free Agent, 2015

YEAR	TEAM	LVL	AGE	PA	R	2B	3B	HR	RBI	BB	K	SB	CS	AVG/OBP/SLG
2016	PUL	RK	18	268	36	10	1	7	25	28	78	10	2	.225/.315/.364
2017	CSC	A	19	389	64	21	5	11	43	41	124	17	7	.297/.373/.483
2017	TAM	A+	19	87	13	2	2	2	14	9	24	6	1	.303/.368/.461
2018	TAM	A+	20	339	45	16	3	3	27	44	87	11	10	.255/.354/.361
2019	NYA	MLB	21	251	25	6	0	6	20	16	92	4	2	.154/.206/.264

Breakout: 6%   Improve: 17%   Collapse: 0%   Attrition: 9%   MLB: 17%
Comparables: Clint Frazier, Anthony Gose, Christian Yelich

With Stanton, Judge, Gardner and Frazier on the roster, it's an understatement to say that the Yankees have an embarrassment of riches in the outfield. What makes it truly a comical statement is when you consider Florial, who had a stunning AZL performance in 2017 and was poised to make the next jump in '18. The paths of prospects are circuitous, though, and Florial's might become more so after undergoing surgery on the hamate bone in his right wrist. You know the old saying with wrist injuries and power, and Florial missed a chunk of development time after being ranked 26th on BP's Top 101 last year. This won't impact his immense speed or the possible impact of his glove in center field, but even still at his young age, Florial needs more reps to nail down his issues with plate discipline and pitch recognition.

YEAR	TEAM	LVL	AGE	PA	DRC+	VORP	BABIP	BRR	FRAA	WARP
2016	PUL	RK	18	268	75	5.1	.305	0.0	CF(43): 0.1, LF(6): -0.8	-0.8
2017	CSC	A	19	389	131	31.8	.431	-0.7	CF(62): -2.1, LF(13): 2.9	1.8
2017	TAM	A+	19	87	121	7.4	.404	0.7	CF(18): 0.4	0.4
2018	TAM	A+	20	339	103	10.5	.353	-0.9	CF(59): 1.8, RF(6): -0.2	0.4
2019	NYA	MLB	21	251	21	-15.2	.216	-0.1	CF 1, LF 0	-1.6

Anthony Seigler C

Born: 06/20/99 Age: 20 Bats: B Throws: S
Height: 6'0" Weight: 200 Origin: Round 1, 2018 Draft (#23 overall)

YEAR	TEAM	LVL	AGE	PA	R	2B	3B	HR	RBI	BB	K	SB	CS	AVG/OBP/SLG
2018	YAT	RK	19	42	7	2	0	1	4	6	7	0	0	.333/.429/.472
2018	PUL	RK	19	53	4	1	0	0	5	8	5	0	0	.209/.340/.233
2019	NYA	MLB	20	251	19	2	0	4	15	16	64	0	0	.112/.169/.179

Breakout: 1%   Improve: 1%   Collapse: 0%   Attrition: 0%   MLB: 1%
Comparables: Francisco Pena, Christian Bethancourt, Brandon Drury

This century, the Yankees have drafted only one first-round position player that produced more than 0.5 WARP, and his name rhymes with fudge. Seigler isn't your typical first-round position player, though. In the age of two-way players, where Shohei Ohtani has set a trend carefully followed by draft prospects like Brendan McKay, he has followed suit… as baseball's first two-way pitcher/catcher. Not only can he do that, but he has somehow merged the powers of Pat Venditte, throwing both 90 mph as a right-hander and a shade lower out of the other hand. While the Yankees have sworn they'll exclusively use him behind the plate, we can dream. What matters most for his long-term prospects is his bat and his actual catching skills—despite how far we've come, the fundamentals are still of the utmost importance. Even if those don't fully hold, a switch-hitting, switch-pitching, catching pitcher is the kind of Rube Goldberg-esque utility player any team would love, and considering the organization's overall track record with these picks, they now have multiple vectors to succeed.

YEAR	TEAM	LVL	AGE	PA	DRC+	VORP	BABIP	BRR	FRAA	WARP
2018	YAT	RK	19	42	176	4.7	.393	-0.3	C(10): -0.2	0.3
2018	PUL	RK	19	53	93	0.4	.231	0.1	C(11): 0.0	0.1
2019	NYA	MLB	20	251	-11	-22.8	.128	-0.5	C 0	-2.5

Troy Tulowitzki SS
Born: 10/10/84   Age: 34   Bats: R   Throws: R
Height: 6'3"   Weight: 205   Origin: Round 1, 2005 Draft (#7 overall)

YEAR	TEAM	LVL	AGE	PA	R	2B	3B	HR	RBI	BB	K	SB	CS	AVG/OBP/SLG
2016	TOR	MLB	31	544	54	21	0	24	79	43	101	1	0	.254/.318/.443
2017	TOR	MLB	32	260	16	10	0	7	26	17	40	0	1	.249/.300/.378
2019	NYA	MLB	34	273	30	12	1	9	34	23	50	1	0	.256/.324/.423

Breakout: 0%   Improve: 24%   Collapse: 16%   Attrition: 8%   MLB: 92%
Comparables: Jhonny Peralta, Miguel Tejada, Edgar Renteria

For this game, we'll need a number—any number. Got it? Okay. Next, pick an adjective. Finally, think of a body part. The weirder, the better. Now, insert those words into this sentence: "Fazed by a career-worst performance in 2017, Troy Tulowitzki sought to reaffirm his place in the starting lineup once more, but was felled by [number] [adjective] [body part] and spent the entirety of his 2018 campaign watching Aledmys Diaz bobble ground balls at short." Rest assured that the words you chose have absolutely no bearing on this story; it's more or less the same one we've seen play out during each of his seasons in Toronto. Sure, he *could* work his way back from season-ending bone spur removal to a full workload in the spring, and sure, he *could* see a resurgence at the plate after three straight years of decline, but we should know better than to put our faith in fairy tales by now.

YEAR	TEAM	LVL	AGE	PA	DRC+	VORP	BABIP	BRR	FRAA	WARP
2016	TOR	MLB	31	544	109	16.6	.272	-1.6	SS(128): 2.8	3.1
2017	TOR	MLB	32	260	85	0.5	.272	-3.0	SS(64): 2.4	0.7
2019	NYA	MLB	34	273	104	11.3	.285	-0.5	SS 2	1.3

Tyler Wade UT

Born: 11/23/94 Age: 24 Bats: L Throws: R
Height: 6'1" Weight: 185 Origin: Round 4, 2013 Draft (#134 overall)

YEAR	TEAM	LVL	AGE	PA	R	2B	3B	HR	RBI	BB	K	SB	CS	AVG/OBP/SLG
2016	TRN	AA	21	583	90	16	7	5	27	66	103	27	8	.259/.352/.349
2017	SWB	AAA	22	388	68	22	4	7	31	38	75	26	5	.310/.382/.460
2017	NYA	MLB	22	63	7	4	0	0	2	5	19	1	1	.155/.222/.224
2018	SWB	AAA	23	408	46	18	4	4	27	37	82	11	8	.255/.328/.360
2018	NYA	MLB	23	70	8	4	0	1	5	4	23	1	0	.167/.214/.273
2019	NYA	MLB	24	37	4	1	0	1	4	3	9	1	0	.212/.278/.333

Breakout: 15%   Improve: 33%   Collapse: 3%   Attrition: 29%   MLB: 53%
Comparables: Matt Duffy, Chase d'Arnaud, Yamaico Navarro

There's always one player who looks like they'd be a much better player on a different team, and for the Yankees, that's Wade. In most worlds he would have gotten more playing time; it seems eons ago that both Aaron Boone and Brian Cashman envisioned him as the everyday second baseman come Opening Day. That lasted just two and a half weeks, as Gleyber Torres supplanted both him and Neil Walker, and even with his ability to play second and shortstop, he played just 36 games at the big league level and hit .167. Though he struggled to find a fit, there is at least some role (or team) that would afford him the opportunity to get more plate appearances, something he needs dearly to become consistent. He's still that same Spring Training player, as mirage-like as that sometimes can be, and his dynamic speed and stellar defense will make him valuable sometime, or somewhere.

YEAR	TEAM	LVL	AGE	PA	DRC+	VORP	BABIP	BRR	FRAA	WARP
2016	TRN	AA	21	583	110	37.6	.317	11.0	SS(91): -5.6, 2B(38): 0.0	2.4
2017	SWB	AAA	22	388	128	30.6	.375	3.0	SS(54): -2.3, 2B(13): 2.8	2.9
2017	NYA	MLB	22	63	65	-3.3	.231	0.7	2B(15): -0.8, SS(7): 0.0	-0.1
2018	SWB	AAA	23	408	97	8.5	.318	-2.1	SS(51): -0.2, LF(12): 2.1	1.1
2018	NYA	MLB	23	70	55	-2.9	.238	1.7	2B(26): -0.6, RF(5): -0.1	-0.1
2019	NYA	MLB	24	37	66	-0.1	.293	0.1	2B 0	0.0

Domingo Acevedo RHP

Born: 03/06/94 Age: 25 Bats: R Throws: R
Height: 6'7" Weight: 250 Origin: International Free Agent, 2012

YEAR	TEAM	LVL	AGE	W	L	SV	G	GS	IP	H	HR	BB/9	K/9	K	GB%	BABIP
2016	CSC	A	22	3	1	0	8	8	42²	34	1	1.5	10.1	48	49%	.308
2016	TAM	A+	22	2	3	0	10	10	50¹	49	3	2.7	9.7	54	42%	.343
2017	TAM	A+	23	0	4	0	7	7	41¹	49	5	2.0	11.3	52	54%	.393
2017	SWB	AAA	23	1	1	0	2	2	12¹	12	0	5.8	5.8	8	35%	.300
2017	TRN	AA	23	5	1	0	14	14	79¹	65	8	1.9	9.3	82	37%	.282
2018	TRN	AA	24	3	3	0	14	10	64²	51	3	2.8	7.2	52	38%	.264
2019	NYA	MLB	25	0	1	0	10	0	10²	11	2	3.5	8.5	10	39%	.293

Breakout: 9%   Improve: 25%   Collapse: 23%   Attrition: 39%   MLB: 58%
Comparables: Joey Lucchesi, Austin Voth, Trevor Richards

Acevedo is nothing short of a physical specimen on the mound, a six-foot-seven behemoth with a triple-digit fastball. That hasn't come with the durability usually afforded to taller pitchers, as he missed most of this season dealing with both blisters and a biceps injury. His high point of the season might be the most symbolic: he earned a promotion to the majors on July 21, only to be sent back down that night, a so-called phantom player. He was removed from the Arizona Fall League roster with an unknown injury, so his 2019 is also in danger of being delayed. He's no longer as young—now entering his age-25 season—so the sun could be setting on his career as a starter. Health is the only thing standing in the way of what is, at bare minimum, a promising future in the back-end of the bullpen.

YEAR	TEAM	LVL	AGE	WHIP	ERA	DRA	WARP	MPH	FB%	WHF	CSP
2016	CSC	A	22	0.96	1.90	1.84	1.7				
2016	TAM	A+	22	1.27	3.22	2.57	1.7				
2017	TAM	A+	23	1.40	4.57	2.28	1.4				
2017	SWB	AAA	23	1.62	4.38	3.79	0.3				
2017	TRN	AA	23	1.03	2.38	2.75	2.3				
2018	TRN	AA	24	1.10	2.92	3.95	1.0				
2019	NYA	MLB	25	1.38	4.77	4.78	0.0				

Roansy Contreras RHP

Born: 11/07/99   Age: 19   Bats: R   Throws: R
Height: 6'0"   Weight: 175   Origin: International Free Agent, 2016

YEAR	TEAM	LVL	AGE	W	L	SV	G	GS	IP	H	HR	BB/9	K/9	K	GB%	BABIP
2017	DYA	RK	17	0	3	0	6	6	22	25	2	2.0	7.0	17	57%	.311
2017	YAN	RK	17	4	1	0	8	5	31^2	35	2	3.4	4.8	17	43%	.297
2018	STA	A-	18	0	0	0	5	5	28^2	15	1	2.8	10.0	32	49%	.219
2018	CSC	A	18	0	2	0	7	7	34^2	29	4	3.1	7.3	28	34%	.255
2019	NYA	MLB	19	2	4	0	10	10	45^2	54	11	4.7	6.5	33	39%	.302

Comparables: Deolis Guerra, Kelvin Herrera, Vicente Campos

Contreras checks off every box for a teenage pitching prospect. Gained weight and started to fill out his frame? Check. Added velocity, up to the mid-90s? Check. A promising change and breaking ball? Check and check. Originally labeled the best Dominican prospect from the 2017 signing period, he is already living up to that title. While he threw in the high-80s to low-90s last season, he has subsequently exploded, and throws in the mid-90s with ease today. He has a plus change and a repeatable delivery. His six-foot and 175 pound frame is not on his side as far as health and durability is concerned, but he hasn't given them a reason to worry just yet. There's a long development road to go, but it fits directly in the mold of a long line of successful international amateurs pumped out of the Yankees' system.

YEAR	TEAM	LVL	AGE	WHIP	ERA	DRA	WARP	MPH	FB%	WHF	CSP
2017	DYA	RK	17	1.36	3.68	4.15	0.4				
2017	YAN	RK	17	1.48	4.26	3.96	0.7				
2018	STA	A-	18	0.84	1.26	3.91	0.4				
2018	CSC	A	18	1.18	3.38	4.40	0.3				
2019	NYA	MLB	19	1.72	6.67	6.78	-0.7				

New York Yankees 2019

Danny Farquhar RHP
Born: 02/17/87 Age: 32 Bats: R Throws: R
Height: 5'9" Weight: 185 Origin: Round 10, 2008 Draft (#309 overall)

YEAR	TEAM	LVL	AGE	W	L	SV	G	GS	IP	H	HR	BB/9	K/9	K	GB%	BABIP
2016	DUR	AAA	29	4	2	2	32	0	38	33	2	2.1	5.7	24	48%	.270
2016	TBA	MLB	29	1	0	0	35	0	35[1]	33	8	3.8	11.7	46	41%	.294
2017	TBA	MLB	30	2	2	0	37	0	35	28	2	5.7	8.5	33	47%	.280
2017	CHR	AAA	30	0	0	1	8	0	9	6	2	2.0	12.0	12	55%	.222
2017	CHA	MLB	30	2	0	0	15	0	14[1]	11	1	3.8	7.5	12	37%	.238
2018	CHA	MLB	31	1	1	0	8	0	8	6	3	0.0	10.1	9	35%	.176
2019	NYA	MLB	32	2	1	0	32	0	34	32	5	4.3	9.4	36	42%	.296

Breakout: 18%   Improve: 38%   Collapse: 19%   Attrition: 10%   MLB: 74%
Comparables: Justin Miller, Fernando Rodriguez, Matt Reynolds

For whatever reason, there's just not a ton of prior precedent in major league baseball about comebacks from ruptured brain aneurysms and the associated near-death experiences that result. While the White Sox and the baseball community has spent the better part of 2018 just being very thrilled that Farquhar is alive after collapsing in the Guaranteed Rate Field home dugout on April 20, the journeyman reliever himself has been pretty set upon the idea of returning to pitching since walking out of the hospital a couple weeks later. Removed from the strain of a professional season for the first time in a decade, Farquhar is throwing harder than ever in his private sessions, but has been back and forth between the majors and Triple-A enough times to know that sticking in a big league bullpen is a battle every year, let alone after a setback of this magnitude.

YEAR	TEAM	LVL	AGE	WHIP	ERA	DRA	WARP	MPH	FB%	WHF	CSP
2016	DUR	AAA	29	1.11	3.32	3.11	0.8				
2016	TBA	MLB	29	1.36	3.06	2.94	0.8	94.7	54.1	15.5	39.9
2017	TBA	MLB	30	1.43	4.11	3.94	0.5	94.5	58.1	14.6	44.1
2017	CHR	AAA	30	0.89	3.00	4.43	0.1				
2017	CHA	MLB	30	1.19	4.40	4.50	0.1	95.0	58.1	11.2	47.9
2018	CHA	MLB	31	0.75	5.62	3.04	0.2	93.9	56.9	16.4	47.1
2019	NYA	MLB	32	1.43	4.68	4.68	0.2	93.6	56.2	14.4	44.3

Luis Gil RHP

Born: 06/03/98 Age: 21 Bats: R Throws: R
Height: 6'3" Weight: 176 Origin: International Free Agent, 2015

YEAR	TEAM	LVL	AGE	W	L	SV	G	GS	IP	H	HR	BB/9	K/9	K	GB%	BABIP
2017	DTW	RK	19	0	2	0	14	14	41^2	31	2	4.3	10.6	49	54%	.287
2018	PUL	RK	20	2	1	0	10	10	39^1	21	1	5.7	13.3	58	35%	.256
2018	STA	A-	20	0	2	0	2	2	6^2	11	1	8.1	13.5	10	39%	.455
2019	NYA	MLB	21	2	3	0	14	7	33^2	35	6	9.2	9.0	34	41%	.309

Comparables: Nestor Cortes, Domingo German, Rafael Montero

Yet another helium prospect from a small deal, this one sending already-designated Jake Cave to Minnesota, Gil has the kind of stuff to make hitters stand and stare, and the kind of command that often rewards them for it. Never a buzzworthy prospect with the Twins, scouts began to take notice as Gil tossed triple-digit fastballs at Pulaski. Combine that with a high-spin curve and you have all of the ingredients for a reliever, at the bare minimum. Throw in a third pitch and more command, and as the thinking goes, there's a mid-rotation starter. For what was essentially a throwaway deal, it's looking more like a heist right about now.

YEAR	TEAM	LVL	AGE	WHIP	ERA	DRA	WARP	MPH	FB%	WHF	CSP
2017	DTW	RK	19	1.22	2.59	3.45	1.2				
2018	PUL	RK	20	1.17	1.37	3.34	1.2				
2018	STA	A-	20	2.55	5.40	3.40	0.1				
2019	NYA	MLB	21	2.06	6.84	6.97	-0.6				

Jordan Montgomery LHP
Born: 12/27/92 Age: 26 Bats: L Throws: L
Height: 6'6" Weight: 225 Origin: Round 4, 2014 Draft (#122 overall)

YEAR	TEAM	LVL	AGE	W	L	SV	G	GS	IP	H	HR	BB/9	K/9	K	GB%	BABIP
2016	TRN	AA	23	9	4	0	19	19	102^1	94	5	3.2	8.5	97	45%	.299
2016	SWB	AAA	23	5	1	0	6	6	37	28	0	2.2	9.0	37	56%	.286
2017	NYA	MLB	24	9	7	0	29	29	155^1	140	21	3.0	8.3	144	42%	.275
2018	NYA	MLB	25	2	0	0	6	6	27^1	25	3	4.0	7.6	23	46%	.282
2019	NYA	MLB	26	2	1	0	5	5	25	25	4	3.7	8.0	22	44%	.293

Breakout: 28% Improve: 56% Collapse: 23% Attrition: 12% MLB: 87%
Comparables: Alex Cobb, Steven Matz, Jake Odorizzi

Would you be able to remember the Rookie of the Year voting from, say, five years ago? Did you know that vote-getters included JB Shuck and David Lough (with more notables like Chris Archer and the winner, Wil Myers)? Jordan Montgomery could be among those forgotten names, appearing out of nowhere to place sixth on the 2017 ballot. His sophomore effort proved a lost year, featuring just 27 1/3 innings, an elbow flexor strain, and the all-too-common Tommy John surgery. Where he goes from there is unknown. Armed with a mere 90 mph fastball, and with the very possible velocity decline most see in recovery, he could find himself unable to cope on just guile and command alone. We'll likely have to wait until 2020 to find out.

YEAR	TEAM	LVL	AGE	WHIP	ERA	DRA	WARP	MPH	FB%	WHF	CSP
2016	TRN	AA	23	1.27	2.55	3.23	2.3				
2016	SWB	AAA	23	1.00	0.97	2.30	1.3				
2017	NYA	MLB	24	1.23	3.88	4.51	1.8	93.4	41.8	12.7	43
2018	NYA	MLB	25	1.35	3.62	5.86	-0.2	91.7	41.1	11	45.3
2019	NYA	MLB	26	1.40	4.47	4.65	0.2	92.7	42.4	12.6	45.1

LINEOUTS

Hitters

HITTER	POS	TEAM	LVL	AGE	PA	R	2B	3B	HR	RBI	BB	K	SB	CS	AVG/OBP/SLG	DRC+	WARP
Josh Breaux	C	STA	A-	20	105	6	9	0	0	13	3	20	0	0	.280/.295/.370	96	-0.2
Antonio Cabello	OF	DYA	Rk	17	30	5	0	1	0	1	6	6	5	1	.227/.433/.318	119	0.1
	OF	YAT	Rk	17	162	21	9	4	5	20	21	34	5	5	.321/.426/.555	193	1.2
Oswaldo Cabrera	2B	CSC	A	19	526	48	24	1	6	48	28	66	4	9	.229/.273/.320	79	0.9
Thairo Estrada	SS	TAM	A+	22	47	4	2	0	0	5	0	9	0	0	.222/.234/.267	52	-0.3
	SS	SWB	AAA	22	34	1	1	0	0	3	0	8	0	0	.152/.176/.182	28	-0.1
Dermis Garcia	1B	CSC	A	20	363	37	17	2	15	50	36	111	3	2	.241/.320/.444	133	0.5
Isiah Gilliam	OF	TAM	A+	21	520	59	22	2	13	71	36	151	4	5	.259/.313/.397	93	-1.3
Ryder Green	OF	YAN	Rk	18	95	11	2	2	3	10	11	35	3	2	.203/.316/.392	78	-0.3
Ryan Lavarnway	C	IND	AAA	30	303	29	23	1	9	33	29	57	0	0	.288/.375/.485	148	1.1
	C	PIT	MLB	30	6	1	1	0	0	1	0	1	0	0	.667/.667/.833	87	0.0
Everson Pereira	CF	PUL	Rk	17	183	21	8	2	3	26	15	60	3	2	.263/.322/.389	68	-0.1
Giovanny Urshela	3B	COH	AAA	26	42	6	4	0	0	7	5	9	0	0	.324/.405/.432	103	0.1
	3B	TOR	MLB	26	46	7	1	0	1	3	2	10	0	0	.233/.283/.326	82	-0.1
	3B	BUF	AAA	26	91	7	3	0	0	5	4	9	0	0	.244/.275/.279	105	0.1
	3B	SWB	AAA	26	107	14	7	2	2	12	4	13	0	0	.307/.340/.475	104	0.3

The Yankees dropped serious cash in the international amateur market, signing four of the top 30 prospects, including Denny Larrondo (29th, $550k), Antonio Gomez (11th, $600k), Osiel Rodriguez (9th, $600k), and **Kevin Alcantara**, who signed for about $1 million. Sporting an above-average arm, plus speed, and a tall frame, he could be a formidable center fielder in a half-decade. ⓧ It's pronounced "Bro," and you know it, because this draft selection was announced by Nick Swisher. **Josh Breaux**, like fellow draftee Anthony Seigler, has pitching ability (to the tune of triple-digits), but hopes will rest on his raw power. ⓧ Venezuelan teenager **Antonio Cabello** moved from catcher to outfield to take advantage of his athleticism, and he put every ounce of it on display in his first stint stateside. He's the kind of prospect that makes prospects fun to track. ⓧ **Oswaldo Cabrera** was an unheralded prospect out of the 2014 international amateur class, and he did little to attract the attention of any nearby heralds. Youth is still on his side and his defense is a plus up the middle, but he still finds himself at the bottom of the offensive rung. ⓧ **Thairo Estrada** easily had the unluckiest season in the organization, both taking a bullet to the hip in a robbery attempt in Venezuela, and then missing most of the season with a back issue. ⓧ When **Dermis Garcia** knocked a few over the wall in a notoriously pitcher-friendly ballpark, it may not have been *spectacular*, per se. But as one of the more high profile 2014 international signings, all eyes will be on 2019, as the Yankees experiment with him as a two-way player. ⚾ **Isiah Gilliam** is part of a historic baseball bloodline; his grandfather, Jim, was the player that took over for Jackie Robinson with the Brooklyn Dodgers. Looking to skyrocket to a starting position on another historic franchise, his switch-hitting power should get him an extended look as he climbs the system. ⚾ **Ryder Green** may sound like the putting grounds of a golf championship, but this baseball name carries a bit more pop. Drafted over-slot in the third round last year, the organization is betting on his plus raw power translating to some long drives. ⚾ A one-time catching prospect thanks to his bat, **Ryan Lavarnway** has spent time in eight organizations over the last four seasons, in part because his defense isn't good enough to survive as a big league backup, but mostly because he keeps telling management "it's Lavarnway or the highway!" everywhere he goes. ⚾ Pegged as one of the top July 2nd amateurs last year and signed for a whopping $1.5 million, **Everson Pereira** completed his first full season with Pulaski, altogether skipping the Dominican Summer League. While the numbers may not be glowing, the reports are, and talk of his tremendous gap power could make him a consensus Top 100 prospect by year's end. ⚾ Now that he's a Yankees third baseman, **Giovanny Urshela** just has to hit a whole bunch of doubles and he'll earn some AL ROY votes.

Pitchers

PITCHER	TEAM	LVL	AGE	W	L	SV	G	GS	IP	H	HR	BB/9	K/9	K	GB%	WHIP	ERA	DRA	WARP
Albert Abreu	TAM	A+	22	4	3	0	13	13	62.2	54	9	4.2	9.3	65	45%	1.32	4.16	4.00	1.0
Daniel Coulombe	NAS	AAA	28	2	1	0	23	1	28.1	30	3	1.9	8.9	28	44%	1.27	2.54	4.09	0.3
	OAK	MLB	28	1	1	0	27	0	23.2	24	5	4.2	9.9	26	56%	1.48	4.56	2.77	0.6
Phillip Diehl	TAM	A+	23	2	2	3	25	0	48.2	37	2	2.2	14.6	79	43%	1.01	3.14	2.34	1.5
	TRN	AA	23	0	1	1	14	0	26.2	18	2	3.7	9.8	29	35%	1.09	1.35	2.49	0.8
J.P. Feyereisen	SWB	AAA	25	6	6	1	37	0	60	56	5	3.8	8.9	59	36%	1.35	3.45	4.84	0.2
Deivi Garcia	CSC	A	19	2	4	0	8	8	40.2	31	5	2.2	13.9	63	31%	1.01	3.76	2.40	1.4
	TAM	A+	19	2	0	0	5	5	28.1	19	0	2.5	11.1	35	37%	0.95	1.27	3.18	0.7
Nolan Martinez	STA	A-	20	4	0	0	8	5	36.2	21	1	2.7	6.4	26	45%	0.87	1.23	7.06	-0.8
	CSC	A	20	0	4	0	5	5	25	24	2	5.0	5.4	15	36%	1.52	6.48	8.27	-0.9
Luis Medina	PUL	Rk	19	1	3	0	12	12	36	32	3	11.5	11.8	47	43%	2.17	6.25	5.38	0.3
Nick Nelson	CSC	A	22	1	1	0	5	5	24.2	18	1	2.6	12.8	35	56%	1.01	3.65	3.49	0.5
	TAM	A+	22	7	5	0	18	17	88.1	69	1	4.8	10.1	99	46%	1.31	3.36	3.22	2.2
	TRN	AA	22	0	0	0	3	3	8.2	10	1	9.3	10.4	10	50%	2.19	5.19	3.89	0.1
Freicer Perez	TAM	A+	22	0	4	0	6	6	25	28	3	6.8	7.2	20	52%	1.88	7.20	4.60	0.2
Matt Sauer	STA	A-	19	3	6	0	13	13	67	60	3	2.4	6.0	45	46%	1.16	3.90	7.29	-1.6
Clarke Schmidt	STA	A-	22	0	1	0	2	2	8.1	4	0	2.2	10.8	10	37%	0.72	1.08	3.04	0.2
Trevor Stephan	TAM	A+	22	3	1	0	7	7	41	23	5	2.0	10.8	49	41%	0.78	1.98	3.33	1.0
	TRN	AA	22	3	8	0	17	17	83.1	80	5	3.1	9.8	91	36%	1.31	4.54	3.90	1.4
Stephen Tarpley	TRN	AA	25	5	0	2	19	0	35.2	18	0	3.8	8.3	33	71%	0.93	1.26	3.47	0.6
	SWB	AAA	25	2	2	0	17	0	34	23	3	2.9	10.1	38	68%	1.00	2.65	3.87	0.5
	NYA	MLB	25	0	0	0	10	0	9	6	0	6.0	13.0	13	52%	1.33	3.00	4.18	0.1
Juan Then	YAN	Rk	18	0	3	0	11	11	50	38	2	2.0	7.6	42	48%	0.98	2.70	5.16	0.5
Garrett Whitlock	CSC	A	22	2	2	0	7	7	40	23	1	1.6	9.9	44	63%	0.75	1.12	3.61	0.8
	TRN	AA	22	1	0	0	2	1	10.2	10	0	5.9	3.4	4	56%	1.59	0.84	5.42	0.0
	TAM	A+	22	5	3	0	14	13	70	60	2	3.5	9.5	74	52%	1.24	2.44	3.98	1.1

After missing Spring Training due to appendix surgery, **Albert Abreu** is starting to look like a major haul in what was a salary dump in the Brian McCann trade. With a sometimes-triple-digits fastball and, overall, three plus pitches, he may be the definition of raw talent, but it's talent nonetheless. ⓧ **Danny Coulombe** suffered the indignity of being designated for assignment in favor of Aaron Brooks in September. He's a pint-size lefty junkballer, which is a lot of fun, except when he falls behind and has to throw his "fast"balls. ⓧ Described as a "command guy" by Trenton Thunder manager Jay Bell, **Phillip Diehl** struggled a bit with said command at Double-A, walking 11 in 36 2/3 innings. That's not awful, though, and he featured sub-3 BB/9 walk rates in every other level of play. There was another unheralded "command guy" who snuck his way on to the big league roster in Jordan Montgomery, and Diehl could be another, albeit in the bullpen, before too long. ⓧ **J.P. Feyereisen**, with his consistent, underwhelming arsenal, isn't just a man destined to ride the bus back and forth from Scranton. He is a bus ride to Scranton. ⓧ Quickly becoming one of the best pitching prospects in the system, **Deivi Garcia** and his high-spin fastball-curve combination cracked Trenton this year. The Yankees are still waiting on the changeup to develop, but his two pitches are major-league ready out of the bullpen. ⚾ Supposedly the more immediate impact arm of the Andrew Miller trade, **Ben Heller** has tossed just 18 total innings, and underwent Tommy John surgery on April 6th. There's no immediacy now, but the team will have 2019 to determine the impact. ⚾ There's a certain ceiling for prospects like **Michael King**, and after a brilliant 2018 campaign, he's pushing against it. A finesse sinkerballer, his stock is at the point where even Brian Cashman admitted that, "We had a ton of requests on him [at the trade deadline]. We had a few teams tell us he would go into their rotation now." ⚾ After missing most of 2017, lean right-hander **Nolan Martinez** finally returned to a full slate of action, picking up a NY-Penn League Player of the Week honor in August. ⚾ In terms of "stuff," **Luis Medina** has what it takes to be an elite big leaguer: mid-to-upper-90s heat, a plus curve, and a developing change that could be a plus in the future as well. There's just no consistency in his delivery. The risk is high with this dynamic 19 year-old, but so is the reward. ⚾ **Nick Nelson** is the definition of a sleeper with raw potential. He features a mid-90s fastball and a solid curve, but with absolutely no command of it. He has been moving up levels, but he will need to add a pitch, and a pinch of command, before he'll see even a cup of coffee. ⚾ Vague injuries are a constant in minor league reporting, and clouds the true direction of a player's development. **Freicer Perez** sits in true prospect limbo after the injury that cost him his 2018 was revealed to be shoulder inflammation. A year removed from rave reviews and Betances comparisons, now we wait for the fog of war to lift. ⚾ The team's 2017 second-rounder, **Matt Sauer** wields a mid-90s fastball, solid command, and a competent slider. With room on his frame for more velocity growth, his realistic floor is another high-powered arm in the bullpen. ⚾ The hardest part of making good on a first-round pick that just went underwent Tommy John surgery is getting through the recovery itself, which ends the careers of a solid chunk of pitchers. Now, the next hardest part for **Clarke Schmidt**: a full season of health. Well, that, and the waiting. ⚾ The Yankees love their fast-rising relievers, and **Trevor Stephan** was drafted in the third round last year to do exactly that. After just one year of development he finds himself knocking on Scranton's door, boasting a curve that could help him avoid same-side work. ⚾ Acquired as the player to be named later in the Ivan Nova trade, **Stephen Tarpley** was called up during roster expansion. A heavy groundball LOOGY isn't in high demand these days, but that one vector will put him among the big league bullpen's arsenal, or at least its reserves. ⚾ A return in the minor Nick Rumbelow deal with Seattle, **Juan Then** put up 11 starts with a 2.70 ERA in the GCL. Entering his age-19 season, and showcasing a fastball near the mid-90s, he's the example of how the Yankees will continue to revitalize their system as they compete: flip players from positions of strength, Then profit. ⚾ A former 18th-round pick, **Garrett Whitlock** continued his methodical rise to the upper minors, flashing that fabled combination of drawing both downward contact and whiffs. While reliever is a likely scenario, thanks to a flimsy third pitch, he'll likely muscle his way into the long Yankee bullpen queue soon.

Yankees Prospects

The State of the System:
The top guys have graduated, leaving a lot of upside and a lot of risk.

The Top Ten:

1. Jonathan Loaisiga   RHP

OFP: 60   Likely: 50   ETA: Debuted in 2018
Born: 11/02/94   Age: 24   Bats: R   Throws: R   Height: 5'11"   Weight: 165
Origin: International Free Agent, 2012

The Report: We thought we were being super aggressive by ranking Loaisiga—at the time a 23-year-old who had one start in full-season ball—as our low-minors sleeper last year. The blurb said he might jump into the "next ten" section of our Yankees list; instead he leapt to the top of the system and into the 101, with a few stops in the majors along the way.

Loaisiga has one of the oddest stories in the minors. He was signed out of Nicaragua by the Giants in 2012, never made it stateside while battling shoulder problems, and was released out of extended spring in 2015. He spent the next year puttering around the fringes of baseball, pitching in his home country's league and for various flavors of the Nicaraguan national team. Yankees scout Ricardo Finol saw him pitch in an international competition and signed Loaisiga early in 2016, just before he was about to depart for a stint in the Italian Baseball League. He finally made his United States debut with a spot start for Low-A Charleston in June 2016, only to immediately suffer an elbow injury that required Tommy John surgery.

Loaisiga popped back up in the late-summer of 2017 like a new man, throwing 95-98 with life and command. The out pitch is a two-plane power breaking ball that usually gets labeled a curve. "Slurve" can sometimes be a pejorative, but not always, and here it's more that he throws a breaking ball with slider velocity and curve movement, which is good. The changeup flashes average and functions as a useful third pitch.

The Risks: Medium, overall. There's high health and relief risk—Loaisiga was hampered in the second half of 2018 by shoulder problems, and with his size and medical history he might be more likely to end up in the bullpen than the rotation. But we think he's reasonably likely to be a Dude in some role.

Bret Sayre's Fantasy Take: It's very tempting to look past Loaisiga, given his health problems and lack of track record. And yet, his command is very intriguing and he showed notable ability to miss bats in the majors during his brief 2018 stint. The contextual factors are always going to be against him, but he was a near miss for me on the Dynasty 101 and a potential SP4 even in that park/division—he just needs to be able to throw the requisite innings.

2. Estevan Florial   OF

OFP: 60   Likely: 50   ETA: Late 2020
Born: 11/25/97   Age: 21   Bats: L   Throws: R   Height: 6'1"   Weight: 185
Origin: International Free Agent, 2015

The Report: Florial is the kind of prospect we love to love. He has all the tools, including plus speed, raw power and arm. The only question is whether he'll hit enough for everything to play.

Seeing him several times this past season, I occasionally got bit of a Byron Buxton vibe. When it all works, things fall in place and it's easy to see the player he can be. When it doesn't, it seems that he struggles to translate any of the tools into consistent production. He did miss about two months in 2018 after surgery on his hamate bone and there was an adjustment period when he returned.

Florial made some changes to his bat path to try to get to more of his power, but he has not yet found the right formula. He knows the strike zone, but he struggles with pitch recognition, which leads to bouts of inconsistency and a good bit of swing and miss. He has also not yet translated his speed into base stealing prowess, as he swiped only 11 bases in 21 attempts last year. While he's no finished product, Florial will only be 21 next year, and players with his raw ability often find a way to make everything work.

The Risks: High. As you might expect, there is more variance with Florial than with most other players in the 101.

Bret Sayre's Fantasy Take: There's no question that Florial is the best dynasty prospect in this system, and the tools still make him someone to value highly. He won't make a repeat appearance as a top-50 fantasy prospect when our list drops later this week, but the upside hasn't gone anywhere—he still can be a .270 hitter with 30-35 bombs if he can tap into that raw talent. He's just a riskier proposition now.

3. Antonio Cabello   OF

OFP: 60   Likely: 50   ETA: 2023
Born: 11/01/00   Age: 18   Bats: R   Throws: R   Height: 5'10"   Weight: 160
Origin: International Free Agent, 2017

The Report: The Yankees spent a boatload in the IFA market for the 2014 J2 class. Almost five years later, the organization's top five prospects are all IFAs, but only Florial—who signed late for a small bonus because of birth certificate issues—was a big ticket signing.

Cabello was signed as a catcher out of Venezuela, and he has the frame of a backstop. That belies his athleticism though and the Yanks quickly moved him out from behind the plate. He's an above-average runner with a chance to stick in center field—despite the rather squat physique—but he may slide over to right.

The bat may very well carry a corner outfield spot though. Cabello has a remarkably advanced hit tool and approach for a 17-year-old. He flashes exceptional barrel control and the ability to drive the ball to the opposite field already, and there's potentially above-average raw power down the line as well. It's very early days for the profile, but Cabello arguably has the most upside in this Yankees system.

The Risks: Extreme. Teenage complex bat learning a new position on the job. Lots of risk here.

Bret Sayre's Fantasy Take: Another tough cut from the 101, Cabello is a player I'll be watching very closely in 2019 to see how his power plays in full-season ball (assuming he gets there). The batting average (and on-base percentage) are the driving forces right now, but it's whether the power/speed can be more than just supplementary that decides Cabello's fantasy fate. If he can ring that future up to 20 apiece, he could slide up into the top 50 fantasy prospects by this time next year.

4

Deivi Garcia   RHP   OFP: 60   Likely: 45   ETA: Late 2019 or 2020
Born: 05/19/99   Age: 20   Bats: R   Throws: R   Height: 5'10"   Weight: 163
Origin: International Free Agent, 2015

The Report: There's a lot going on here. Garcia made his Double-A debut just three months after his 19th birthday, after buzzing through A-ball with ease. He throws in the low-to-mid-90s, and the party piece is one of the better curveballs in the minors. We can say here what we can't always say publicly elsewhere: Garcia has an extremely high spin rate, and we can confirm that on the record because the Yankees have said it themselves.

What to make of that as evaluators is something we struggle with right now—teams have much greater access to spin rate data than we do, and they have a fuller data set to contextualize it; we get ours anecdotally and less reliably. Garcia's curveball would rank towards the top of the MLB spin rate chart, and that is generally a good thing. But we also don't need that data to project it as a potential plus-plus pitch, either: it's a sharp swing-and-miss breaker that he commands well, which is obvious in any viewing of him.

Our major concern here is that Garcia has never thrown more than the 74 innings he tossed in 2018. He's short and slight of frame, and the Yankees held him back until June in extended spring training. It's a tough projection right now to get him to a MLB starting workload. Not impossible, but tough.

The Risks: High on durability, low on talent.

Bret Sayre's Fantasy Take: It really is a shame that the highest-upside arm in this system is such a bad bet to pitch enough innings to capitalize on that talent. A better frame would make him a top-101 arm, but the reliever risk here makes him both a potential SP3 and barely a top-150 fantasy prospect.

5. Everson Pereira   OF
OFP: 55   Likely: 45   ETA: 2022-23
Born: 04/10/01   Age: 18   Bats: R   Throws: R   Height: 6'0"   Weight: 191
Origin: International Free Agent, 2017

The Report: We're usually somewhat conservative with recent international signings, until they've established themselves outside of a complex. Pereira jumped the complex league level completely and made his pro debut at the tender age of 17 in the Appalachian League. He's even *younger* than Wander Franco, who did the same thing to much greater fanfare.

Pereira isn't quite Franco in terms of impact tools, and he was more fine-to-good in the Appy than great. It's a solid profile—good natural hitting ability, plus runner, goes and gets it in center field—without screaming superstar potential. There's projectability in the body, and he might yet grow into some real power, although it isn't there yet and there's a lot of weight on "might" there. But having a decent season stateside at that age is a huge accomplishment, worthy of substantial praise in and of itself.

The Risks: Medium-to-high. There are enough secondary skills here that we think he's got a strong shot to make it as 17-year-old short-season players go, but the shape of it all is still very uncertain.

Bret Sayre's Fantasy Take: It's still too early to go too far in on Pereira, but he's a great name to keep an eye on in 2019 as a potential riser. Right now it's more of a speed-based OF3 profile, but it is still awfully early. He should be owned if your league rosters 200 prospects.

6. Luis Gil   RHP
OFP: 55   Likely: 45   ETA: 2022
Born: 06/03/98   Age: 21   Bats: R   Throws: R   Height: 6'3"   Weight: 176
Origin: International Free Agent, 2015

The Report: We like Jake Cave at Baseball Prospectus. He's a nifty fourth outfielder who might've added enough pop to be a platoon guy or even a regular now. But he was once Rule 5'd, and the Yankees pretty much had to move him last spring in a roster crunch. In return for Cave, the Yanks got Gil, a tall drink of water right out of the Twins' Dominican complex. He throws in the mid-to-upper-90s with ease, along with a potentially useful curveball and a fringy changeup. The command isn't there yet, but he was one of the more impressive pitchers in the Appy League, and has a chance to be an impact arm in three or four years. The Yankees have repeatedly stolen unheralded players out of the low levels of other systems. These moves are a testament to both their scouting and player development operations, which power a strong farm system that never gets to add premium talent in the draft.

The Risks: Extreme, and this is one of those guys I'd write as a 70/30 if it was sensible to do so. Gil has never even thrown as many as 50 innings in a season, is extremely wild, and missed the entire 2017 season with arm problems. There's durability risk, relief risk, injury risk, performance risk, all of it.

Bret Sayre's Fantasy Take: If you're in a deep league and want to bet on arm strength, he's a good risk to take, but in most formats you can sit back on players like this until they've got a little more stateside experience. There are just so many short-season arms you can dream of as potential SP2s if everything clicks.

7. Mike King   RHP

OFP: 55   Likely: 45   ETA: Late 2019
Born: 05/25/95   Age: 24   Bats: R   Throws: R   Height: 6'3"   Weight: 210
Origin: Round 12, 2016 Draft (#353 overall)

The Report: King is another great example of the organization's scouting strength. While certainly serviceable in Miami's system, King grew tremendously in his first season with the Yankees, moving through three levels and finding success throughout. The foundation for that success is both physical and mental. He has a plus sinker that he throws at 91-93 with good movement. He uses that offering to generate ground balls. King adds plus command and control to that and he has also shown an ability to read hitters and make adjustments from pitch to pitch.

The biggest shortcoming to this point has been an inability to come up with another plus secondary offering or two to pair with the two-seamer. He made progress this season with his slider, but it's not reliably a swing-and-miss pitch yet. He is also working to add a four-seam fastball and a changeup. Both pitches are slightly behind the slider.

King doesn't hurt himself, keeps the ball in the park, and has shown the ability to succeed even as he has been promoted aggressively. In a system bursting with toolsy but volatile prospects, King stands out as a high-probability big-leaguer, even if his ceiling is a bit lower than most of the names surrounding him on this list.

The Risks: Medium. There is always an injury risk with any pitcher, but King's command/control gives him minimal non-injury risk.

Bret Sayre's Fantasy Take: Innings eaters have value to big-league teams, but dynasty owners just have different priorities. There isn't enough ability to miss bats for us to pay much attention here.

8. Roansy Contreras   RHP

OFP: 55   Likely: 45   ETA: 2022ish
Born: 11/07/99   Age: 19   Bats: R   Throws: R   Height: 6'0"   Weight: 175
Origin: International Free Agent, 2016

The Report: Last year, we wrote up Contreras as a low-90s guy with a chance to reach the mid-90s. Fast forward, and he's already there and looking pretty advanced for a teenager. His changeup flashes plus. The curveball isn't far behind. It's a pretty good arm action with good command for the level. He's got a nice smooth delivery and repeats well. He's a bit on the slight/small side for now, but there's some physical projectability remaining. I hope you aren't sick of reading about this type of arm, because there are like a half-dozen more ahead.

About that last point: we aren't, strictly speaking, supposed to care about organizational development track records and that sort of thing. On our national products and grades, we generally treat a Yankees pitching prospect the same as an Orioles one. Yet we can't help but note that the Yankees track record of developing pitchers of this type is as good as anyone else in the game. That already shows up in the system depth. The Yankees are perceived to have a farm system that is "down" right now because they've graduated or traded most of their high-end talent, but the arms at this end of the list are awfully good for the back of a Top Ten.

The Risks: High, simply because he's a slight of frame kid who just turned 19 and has made five starts above short-season ball. But on the lower side of high.

Bret Sayre's Fantasy Take: It's very clear at this point the Yankees have a type, and unfortunately it doesn't align with the type that dynasty owners have.

9. Clarke Schmidt   RHP

OFP: 55   Likely: 45   ETA: 2020
Born: 02/20/96   Age: 23   Bats: R   Throws: R   Height: 6'1"   Weight: 200
Origin: Round 1, 2017 Draft (#16 overall)

The Report: I wrote Joe Palumbo up for the Next Year's 101 article under the theory that interesting pitchers often make big jumps the year after returning from Tommy John surgery. One of the other pitchers I strongly considered for that "slot" was Clarke Schmidt. Ultimately, Palumbo had more of a pro track record both before and after surgery, but Schmidt has appeal too: a righty who slings in a heavy fastball in the mid-90s, projects for an easy plus slider, a changeup that also flashes pretty big, and even gives you a show-me curve. And we know the Yankees quite like him, because they drafted Schmidt in the middle of the first round in 2017 even though he'd *already had* surgery earlier that spring.

It takes about two calendar years, give or take, for command and feel to fully return after UCL replacement surgery, and there are often bumps in the road, especially that first year. Schmidt made his pro debut this past June, and was handled extremely carefully, making eight abbreviated starts in the GCL and NYPL. We're going to need to see him make 20-plus starts and throw fuller games before we go crazy here, but early returns were pretty good. He could move quite fast if things fall right, a la Loaisiga.

The Risks: High. We have no idea yet if Schmidt can handle a pro starting workload, although there's probably a fastball/slurve reliever here even if things don't work out. Early signs on his return were promising, but there have been pitchers who haven't made the next step. There's also some positive risk here—the possibility that the injury was hiding his full talent.

Bret Sayre's Fantasy Take: I'd let someone else take the risk here and use the roster spot on someone who's not a pitcher.

10 Chance Adams   RHP
OFP: 55   Likely: 45   ETA: Debuted in 2018
Born: 08/10/94   Age: 24   Bats: R   Throws: R   Height: 6'1"   Weight: 220
Origin: Round 5, 2015 Draft (#153 overall)

The Report: Are the days of a fastball up to 98 and a plus-plus slider coming back here? Adams battled elbow problems for much of the season amidst sagging velocity, and was most often 91-94 instead of the 93-96 you'd see at his best. He didn't pitch nearly as well in Triple-A as he'd done in 2017, although he did account fairly well for himself during an emergency start in Fenway in August.

Adams always had significant relief risk; he was a college reliever whom the Yankees converted to starting in 2016. His changeup and curveball are underdeveloped compared to the rest of the profile, and now injuries have taken hold and affected his stuff and command for most of a season. It really is an explosive fastball/slider combo when things are working well, and if the stuff doesn't come all the way back this spring, it might be time to start considering a shift back to the bullpen.

The Risks: High. Health and durability are major concerns at this point.

Bret Sayre's Fantasy Take: You know what we do with likely relievers here. This is the 30th list after all.

The Next Five:

11 Anthony Seigler   C
Born: 06/20/99   Age: 20   Bats: B   Throws: S   Height: 6'0"   Weight: 200
Origin: Round 1, 2018 Draft (#23 overall)

Pat Venditte has nothing on Anthony Seigler, an athletic switch-hitting catcher with the potential to play other left-spectrum positions. Oh, and he was also a real prospect as a switch-pitcher too.

The Yankees popped the Florida prep in the first round and placed him behind the plate, while noting there might be other possibilities down the line. The bat is fairly advanced, with a sweet-looking, quick swing and a decent idea at the plate. The power projection is another thing still more in the line of possibility than actualization yet. As we frequently note, the history of high school catching prospects is terrible, between the amount of development needed and the pressure put on by the rigor of the position, but Seigler is too interesting not to rank. And hey, putting him eleventh saves us having to come up with a full grade and risk profile for another year.

12 Albert Abreu   RHP
Born: 09/26/95   Age: 23   Bats: R   Throws: R   Height: 6'2"   Weight: 175
Origin: International Free Agent, 2013

It was a rough year for our former two-time top 101 guy. Abreu missed the first month of the season after having his appendix removed, disappeared for another month later in the season with elbow problems, and didn't pitch well when he toed the rubber. The lost 2018 came after he missed much of 2017 with recurring shoulder problems, so durability is now a major red flag. We needed to see a command jump here if he had much of a chance to stay in the rotation long-term anyway, and that hasn't come yet either. He hasn't fallen quite as much as "101 to off the top ten" suggests, because we're still in the OFP 55 projection range here. The hourglass has started running, but there's still a mid-to-upper-90s fastball and power curve combination to be reckoned with lurking deeper.

13 Luis Medina   RHP
Born: 05/03/99   Age: 20   Bats: R   Throws: R   Height: 6'1"   Weight: 175
Origin: International Free Agent, 2015

Medina ratchets it up to the upper-90s freely and easily, his curveball projects as a future plus swing-and-miss offering, and his changeup might get to average or fringe-average eventually. We've talked about how deep the system is, sure. Even still, why is he down here in the next five with that kind of raw stuff? Simply put, his command and control are terrible at present, and "terrible" might be generous. Medina walked 46 batters in 36 innings in the Appy League this year, which is genuinely difficult to do when you have that kind of stuff in short-season ball. The arm is special enough that he's going to have a bunch of chances to pull it together in various roles, but there's much to assemble here.

14 Frank German   RHP
Born: 09/22/97   Age: 21   Bats: R   Throws: R   Height: 6'2"   Weight: 195
Origin: Round 4, 2018 Draft (#127 overall)

The Yankees have a long history (*gesticulates wildly at the rest of the list*) of developing low-investment arms into significant prospects. One particular type of pitcher they gravitate towards here are southeastern college pitchers. They popped German in the fourth round last year, after a fine career as a starter at the University of North Florida. He came out with a typical fourth-round college starter profile: low-90s fastball, nice breaking ball, decent change, good command; a prospect but not a particularly exciting one. Of course, since it's the Yankees, his velocity almost immediately spiked into the mid-90s and touched

98 as a pro in the Penn League. He was pitching in relatively short stints, up to only four innings and 55 pitches, and he spent the summer of 2017 in relief on the Cape. In other words, he might be a pen guy, which is why we aren't quite going nuts yet, but if he retains these gains in true starting length stints in full-season, he's going to shoot up this list quite fast.

15 Josh Stowers OF
Born: 02/25/97   Age: 22   Bats: R   Throws: R   Height: 6'1"   Weight: 200
Origin: Round 2, 2018 Draft (#54 overall)

Stowers was the Mariners second-round pick this past summer, and the Yankees picked him up in the Sonny Gray/Shed Long three-way deal. We have him rated lower than we rated Shed despite an intriguing power/speed combo and a two-year track record of college performance at Louisville. That part of the deal still makes sense for the Yankees, since Stowers is years away from the 40-man and the Yankees love their athletic outfielders and college performers. Despite present above-average speed, Stowers might end up in a corner—likely left due to a fringy arm. And we don't know how much of that power will get into games against better pitching yet. This is one of those profiles where it may just come down to how many sliders he can lay off, and we didn't learn anything more about that in the Northwest League than we did in the ACC. There's a potential average hit/power every day center fielder there, with a likelier outcome as a bench outfielder.

Others of note:

Josh Breaux, C, Short-season Staten Island

Hall of Fame football coach Bill Parcells had a draft philosophy, which Bill Belichick has copied, where he'd sometimes double-up positions with high picks. This makes intrinsic sense: if you want one really good running back, you have better odds if you draft Butch Woolfork *and* Joe Morris instead of just one of them (the really good one ended up being Joe Morris). This doesn't typically translate to baseball since roles are flexible enough that you don't need to slot guys that tightly at draft time. But catcher is really off to the side on the defensive spectrum, its own little thing with its own little quirks, and the attrition rate is high enough that you're probably going to need to have multiple real prospects donning the tools of ignorance.

Breaux represents that rare double-up, coming in the second round of last year's draft after Seigler went in the first. Like Seigler, he was also a significant prospect on the mound, and there's probably fallback potential there if things don't work out at the plate. There's huge raw power here and thus big upside, but he needs to make significant refinements to his hitting approach if he's going to get there in games, and his defense behind the plate needs work too.

Domingo Acevedo, RHP, Double-A Trenton

Acevedo slipping off the top ten saved us from having to deal with a weird quirk in his ETA—he's been on an MLB roster, called up to serve in an emergency depth role during last season's Subway Series, but he's yet to actually pitch in the majors. He was only intermittently healthy in 2018, missing about six weeks early in the season with blister issues, suffering a concussion while already on the DL, and losing almost a month late in the summer with a bicep strain. He also didn't advance past Double-A, a level he'd already conquered in 2017. With a violent delivery, strong starting system depth, and pre-existing inconsistency, he could be pushed to the bullpen forever any minute now. The fastball and slider are big enough that it still could be a heck of a relief outcome, though.

Trevor Stephan, RHP, Double-A Trenton

Stephan has a weird arm action—he drops late from what looks like a standard overhand or high-3/4 look to a low-3/4 slot. That type of slot isn't always a bullpen profile, but it usually isn't very deceptive to lefties without a strong third pitch to the armside, and Stephan's changeup isn't tracking to get there. He does have a strong two-pitch mix up front with a mid-90's fastball and a frisbee slider, and we wouldn't be shocked if those pop a little more in short relief down the road. If this all sounds like the profile for a righty reliever who mows down same-side hitters, well, you're probably on the right path.

Thairo Estrada, IF

The Yankees have a cast of thousands that we could've written about down here, some of whom might project as bigger prospects than Estrada. He *is* worth talking about on his talent alone, but he also earned a mention for reasons bigger than baseball. Estrada was shot in the hip last offseason during a robbery in his native Venezuela, and he had a brutally complicated recovery that caused him to miss most of the 2018 season. Before the injury, he was a cool hit-tool driven sleeper middle infielder hidden in a deep system. He got back on the field more consistently in the Arizona Fall League, and we'll have a better handle on what he is moving forward in the spring. The Yankees have retained him on the 40-man roster through it all, and it would be a fantastic thing if he can establish himself as a MLB player.

Top Talents 25 and Under (born 4/1/93 or later):

1. Gleyber Torres
2. Miguel Andujar
3. Luis Severino
4. Clint Frazier
5. Jonathan Loaisiga

6. Estevan Florial
7. Antonio Cabello
8. Deivi Garcia
9. Jonathan Holder
10. Tyler Wade

Gleyber Torres came into his full game power right when he hit the majors, and quickly established himself as one of baseball's best young infielders. We use "infielders" instead of "shortstops" because his position isn't quite clear yet over the short-term or the long-term, with a lot of moving parts around New York's infield. He played most of 2018 at second base and excelled there, but he's also fine at shortstop and has experience at third base.

One of those moving pieces ranks just below Torres here. Miguel Andujar had a phenomenal rookie season at the plate, nearly stealing Rookie of the Year honors away from Shohei Ohtani. He wasn't so good in the field at third base, and his poor throwing accuracy had a cascading effect on his all around his game. He could be headed to first base or designated hitter sooner rather than later, possibly as soon as this year.

Luis Severino was just ahead of Torres last year, and would've been at the top of this exercise had we done it in the first half of the season. Even with the terrible second half, he was still one of the better pitchers in the American League overall. He's an ace, albeit one with a touch of risk built in.

You probably don't know what to make of Clint Frazier. I don't either. He's had terrible concussion issues—ones that wrecked his life not just on the baseball field but off it too—and we aren't equipped to project how that impacts him moving forward. Given what he was battling, his 2018 performance at Triple-A is nothing short of remarkable, and the underlying tools here have always been amazing. Let's hope it comes back together for him in 2019.

Sneaking onto the bottom of the list are Jonathan Holder and Tyler Wade. Holder has pretty much solidified himself as a quality setup relief option on skill, who the Yankees will likely continue to use in middle relief because of the depth of their bullpen. Wade's in that weird ineligible for lists/still basically a prospect zone, just 24 and likely headed back to Triple-A for the start of 2019. He hasn't come into the power we thought he had a shot at yet, and he hasn't hit in the majors at all in limited opportunities, but he has retained most of the skills that got him onto the rear of the top 101 two years ago. He deserves a shot to be someone's bench weapon sooner rather than later; the Yankees seem to have blocked him with DJ LeMahieu and Troy Tulowitzki over the short term, unfortunately.

New York Yankees 2019

Just as the cherry on top, Aaron Judge, Gary Sanchez, and Greg Bird are all ineligible for this list by less than a year. What a crop of young talent, for the franchise that already has the largest economic advantages in the sport.

Part 3: Featured Articles

The Hole in The Shift is Fixing Itself

Russell Carleton

I've been on a bit of a mission against The Shift of late. I'm not out to get The Shift for the usual reasons that people oppose it. The words "the right way to play the game" won't be found on my lips. If a team wants to pursue a strategy that is within the rules and it works, then by all means, they have my blessing (not that they need it). Instead, my concern with The Shift is a worry that it doesn't work, or at least that it has a flaw that needs fixing.

The data show that while The Shift does a decent job of preventing singles on balls in play (what it's supposed to do), it also increases the number of walks that happen in front of it, and the number of additional walks outweighs the number of singles saved. It's a problem because you can't throw a guy out if he gets to walk to first base.

But the "why" was important. It seemed that The Shift was changing the way in which pitchers pitched. We saw that there were fewer fastballs thrown in front of The Shift than we might otherwise expect, and that pitchers tended to stay out of the strike zone a little more. Not by a lot. In fact, it might not even be visible to the naked eye. The percentage of pitches that are out of the zone goes from 51.0 to 53.3 from a standard defense (two right/two left) to a full shift (three on one side). That difference stands up even after we control for the types of hitters that get shifted against. And it's enough to drive up the walk rate to where it cancels out the benefits that teams thought they were getting with The Shift… and then some.

But there was some hope. I found that when individual pitchers stayed closer to the in-zone/out-of-zone mix that they used without The Shift on, they could still get the benefits of The Shift without the walk problems. So, in theory, a team could simply figure out a way to convince its pitchers to not fall prey to the walk trap and The Shift would once again be their friend.

It's reasonable to think that some teams might be more hip to this idea than others. Maybe some figured it out a year before the others. Maybe they were better at getting the message across to their pitchers. Or, maybe no one has figured it out yet.

Warning! Gory Mathematical Details Ahead!

I used data from 2015-2017, made available through MLB's data portal, Baseball Savant. They are kind enough to note when teams are using an infield shift (three fielders on one side of second base), as opposed to a "strategic shift" (someone's playing a bit out of position, but it's not quite that drastic) or a "standard" alignment.

Since we're doing this by team, I can't just look at raw walk rates, because we know that some teams have good pitchers and others have not-so-good pitchers. Some have a mix of both. I used the log-odds ratio method to take into account a batter's general walking proclivities, and a pitcher's as well, and then shoving them into a binary logistic regression. Then, I asked the computer to generate a specific coefficient for each team's pitchers, for when they went into The Shift and how that affected their walk rate.

Using those coefficients, I was able to project what would happen if a league-average pitcher faced a league-average hitter (which we expect would product a league-average walk rate; from 2015-2017, 7.7 percent of plate appearances ended in a walk) and then just switched his hat. Here's the top five and the bottom five:

Top 5 Teams	Projected Shift Walk Rate	Bottom 5 Teams	Projected Shift Walk Rate
Rockies	6.2%	Rangers	11.2%
Pirates	6.7%	Mets	10.4%
Indians	7.2%	Dodgers	10.2%
Astros	7.3%	Cardinals	9.9%
Braves	7.7%	Tigers	9.7%

There are probably people out there right now trying to figure out what the common thread is among the top and bottom teams. I'm sure, because this is Baseball Prospectus, people are already trying to make the case that sabermetric "early adopters" have some sort of edge here. I think that the more interesting piece is that by the time you get to fifth place in The Shift, we're at league average.

As a sanity check, I examined the issue on a pitch-by-pitch level, looking at how often pitchers threw their pitches in the GameDay strike zone, and again using the same basic methodology and getting team-specific coefficients. The names on the list re-arranged themselves, but the idea was the same, and the two lists correlated with an R of .593.

There's a reason that I don't usually do this type of leaderboard post. I don't really know what the Rockies, Pirates, Indians, Astros, and Braves have in common, or what they have that the bottom five don't. I can put a shrug emoji here and say, "Well, it must be something!" but that seems like a cop-out. Instead, I'd like to present another table and suggest that the table above doesn't even really matter anymore.

Year	League Percent Outside K Zone (Full Shift)	League Percent in K Zone (No Shift)	Difference
2015	54.1%	51.1%	3.0%
2016	53.3%	50.9%	2.4%
2017	52.6%	50.9%	1.7%
2018	52.0%	50.7%	1.3%

The hole in The Shift is fixing itself, and it's coming down really fast league wide. In my earlier work on The Shift, I suggested that until teams stopped having such a huge difference between their out-of-zone rate with and without The Shift on, there would just be too many walks for The Shift to make sense. It seems that all 30 of them have been working toward just that. I once estimated that it takes about 10 years for an idea to filter its way through baseball. At this rate, it looks like teams are going to catch up a lot faster than that. And yeah, they're all saber-smart now.

It's likely that whatever magic it was that the Rockies and Pirates had has made its way to Texas and Queens. Or is at least on its way. And if teams are committing to fixing the walk problem, then it's likely that they will continue shifting and shifting a lot.

And eventually it's going to actually make sense for them to do it.

—*Russell Carleton is a former author of Baseball Prospectus and now an analyst for the New York Mets.*

The State of the Quality Start

Rob Mains

One of the seven things you (probably) didn't know about the 2018 season is that quality starts—defined as a start lasting six or more innings with three or fewer earned runs allowed—as a percentage of total starts cratered to an all-time low of 41 percent. I want to look a little more deeply into this, since it's been a while (May of 2016, to be exact) since I've examined quality starts.

The term *quality start* is credited to *Philadelphia Inquirer* sportswriter John Lowe. It's been derided ever since he coined it in December of 1985. Three runs in six innings? That's a 4.50 ERA! In what world is that a measure of quality?

Let's start with that criticism. It's true that 3 x 9 / 6 = 4.5. (You came here for this sort of high-level math, right?) But it's also true that type of start, meeting the bare minimum for earning a quality start, is unusual. Here's the proportion of quality starts in which the pitcher lasted exactly six innings and yielded exactly three earned runs. (I'm going to confine this analysis to the 30-team era, 1998-present. Almost all data retrieved in this article is via the Baseball-Reference Play Index.)

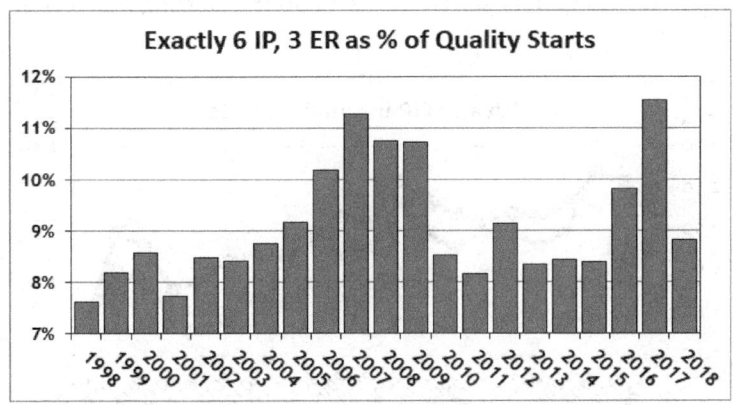

There were 1,997 quality starts in 2018. Only 176, or fewer than one in 11, featured a pitcher going six innings and allowing three earned runs. Put another way, the percentage of quality starts that resulted in a 4.50 ERA (8.8 percent) is less than half the percentage of games in which a batter hit two home runs and his team lost (22.5 percent; 237-69 won-lost). That doesn't impugn hitting two homers.

So if a 4.50 ERA isn't the norm, what is? How good are quality starts?

Pretty good, it turns out. First, on a team level:

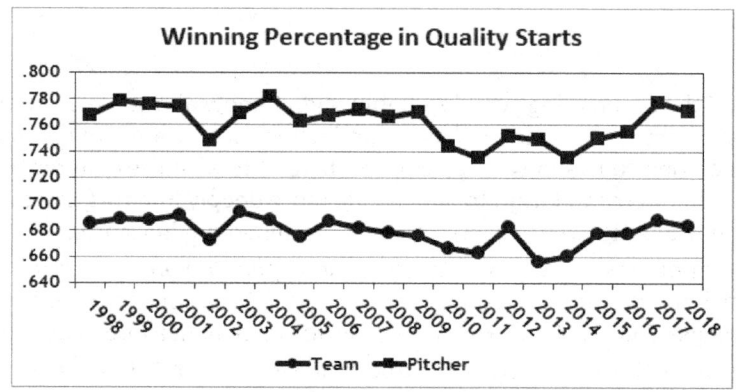

Teams receiving a quality start from their pitcher won 68.4 percent of their games in 2018, in line with the 30-team era average of 67.9 percent. A team with a .684 winning percentage wins 111 games. Getting a quality start is definitely a good thing. Individual pitchers throwing quality starts have a higher winning percentage because a big slice of team losses is assigned to a reliever.

If teams do well in quality starts, how well do the starting pitchers do? Again, very well.

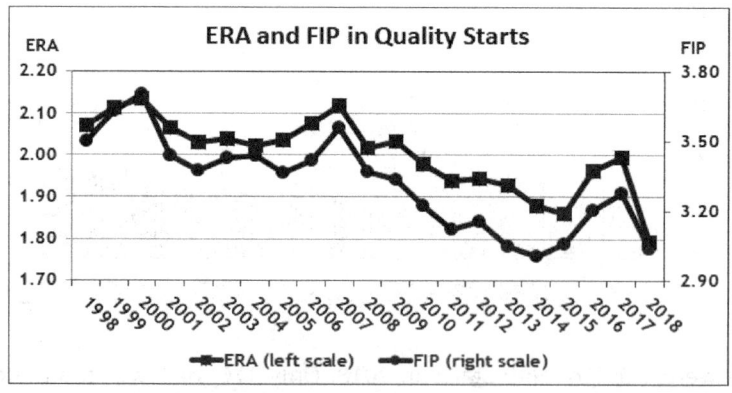

Pitchers in quality starts had a 1.79 ERA (blue line) in 2018, *the lowest in the 30-team era*. Their FIP was higher, 3.04, but still excellent. In the 30-team era, only 2014 had a lower FIP for quality starts, 3.01.

But, of course, the run environment in 2014 was different. Teams in 2014 scored 4.07 runs per game, the fewest in a non-strike year since 1976. They scored 4.45 runs per game in 2018. So surrendering a 3.04 FIP in 2018 is more impressive than 3.01 in 2014. Accordingly, let's look at ERA and FIP in quality starts relative to league averages.

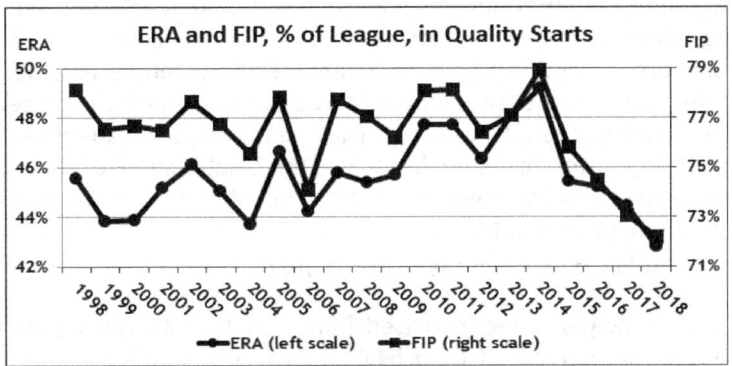

This tells a more dramatic story. Starting pitchers in 2018 gave up a 4.19 ERA and a 4.21 FIP. Starters in quality starts gave up a 1.79 ERA, 43 percent of the league average. Starters in quality starts gave up a 3.04 FIP, 72 percent of the league average. Both of these marks represent lows in the 30-team era.

The takeaway here is this: *Quality starts are better, relative to other starts, than they've ever been over the past 21 years.*

Maybe during the winter I'll look at this over a longer arc of time. For now, though, we can definitively say quality starts are the best they've ever been since the Diamondbacks and Rays joined the majors.

Yet, paradoxically, they're down.

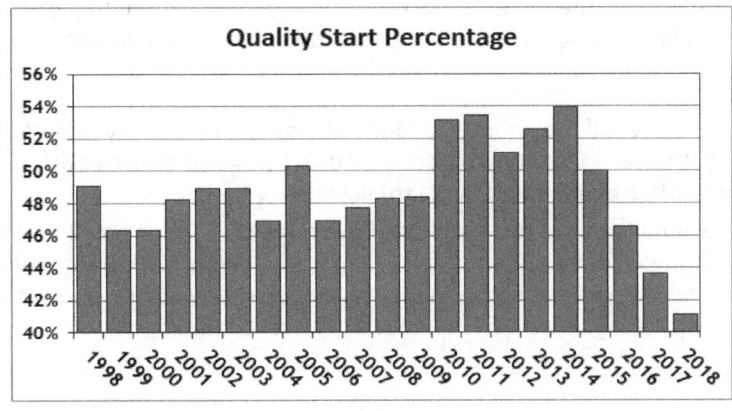

This graph covers only the 30-team era. In my article last week, though, I looked at the years 1908-2018. The result was the same. The 41 percent of starts in 2018 that were quality starts are an all-time low, well below the runners-up: 1930's 43 percent (the year teams scored an all-time record 5.55 runs per game) and last year's 44 percent.

The normal explanation for a dip in quality start percentage is an increase in scoring. When teams score a lot of runs, it's harder for starting pitchers to last six or more innings and limit opponents to three earned runs. From 1998 to 2014, the correlation between runs scored per game and the percentage of starts that were quality starts was -0.94. That means there was an extremely close relationship: More runs, fewer quality starts. Too small a sample? Go back to the start of the Expansion Era, 1961, and the relationship is even more negative, a -0.95 correlation, though 2014.

But that's broken down over the past four years:

- 2015: Runs per game increased from 4.07 to 4.25, quality start percentage decreased from 54.0 to 50.1. Yes, that's a negative relationship, but the regression model would predict a decline of 1.5 percentage points. We got 3.9 instead.
- 2016: Runs per game increased from 4.25 to 4.48, quality start percentage decreased from 50.1 to 46.6. Past experience would suggest a decline of just 1.8 percentage points. We got 3.4.
- 2017: Runs per game increased from 4.48 to 4.65, quality start percentage decreased from 46.6 to 43.6. Again, the direction's right, but the magnitude isn't. Using the relationship from 1998 to 2014, that increase in scoring should've reduced quality starts by 1.3 percentage points, not 2.9.
- 2018: Runs per game declined from 4.65 to 4.45. That should've resulted in the quality start percentage moving in the other direction, rising 1.6 points. It didn't. It fell 2.6 points, as noted, to an all-time low.

Granted, we're talking about just four years here. Maybe they're outliers. But I don't think they are. Quality starts, as noted, are as good or better than ever. But they're rarer than ever as well. And I think I know why.

To get a quality start, you need to allow three or fewer earned and pitch at least six innings. That's 18 outs. Here's a graph showing the number of starting pitchers who limited their opponents to three or fewer earned runs but got pulled after pitching at least five innings but fewer than six:

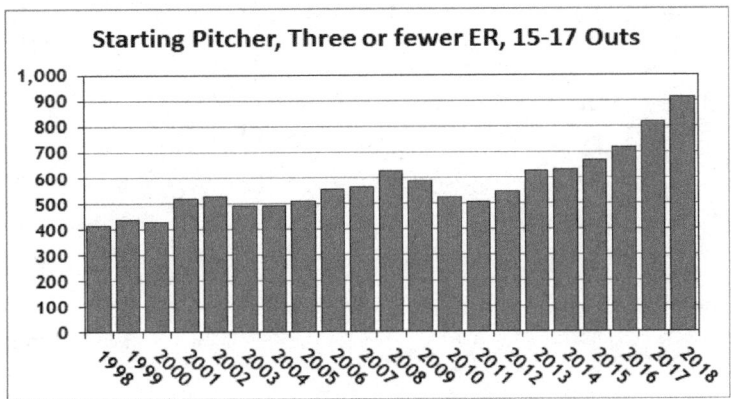

A pitcher getting 15 outs pitched five innings. A pitcher getting 16 outs pitched 5 1/3. A pitcher getting 17 outs pitched 5 2/3. More than ever before, pitchers are being removed from games in which they are within 1-3 outs of a quality start, falling just short of the six-inning finish line. Widespread acknowledgement of the times-through-the-order penalty and a flotilla of available bullpen arms is making the quality start simultaneously both more excellent and more rare.

Which is ironic, given that we saw a new post-war quality start record this season:

Rank	Pitcher	Season	Consecutive QS
1	Jacob deGrom	2018	24
2	Bob Gibson	1968	22
-	Chris Carpenter	2005	22
4	Johan Santana	2004	21
5	Luis Tiant	1968	20
-	Mike Scott	1986	20
-	Jake Arrieta	2015	20
8	Robin Roberts	1952	19
-	Tom Seaver	1973	19
-	Jack Morris	1983	19
-	Greg Maddux	1998	19
-	Josh Johnson	2010	19
-	Jon Lester	2014	19

While there have been longer streaks spread over multiple seasons, no pitcher since World War II threw more consecutive quality starts in one year than Jacob deGrom this year. The fact that he did in a year in which quality starts were the rarest they've ever been adds to the accomplishment.

—*Rob Mains is an author of Baseball Prospectus.*

Heads-Up Hacking—The First Pitch

Matthew Trueblood

Batters fell behind in a higher percentage of all plate appearances in 2018 than in any previous season for which we have pitch-by-pitch data. That kind of granular information goes back only to 1988, but we might safely assume (given all we know about baseball as it had been before that, and as it has been in the years since) that batters have *never* fallen behind at a higher rate than they did last season.

Through the 1990s, the percentage of all plate appearances that began 0-1 hovered in the high 30s and low 40s. In the 2000s, it rose steadily but slowly, through the mid-40s. In 2018, 49.8 percent of all trips to the plate began 0-1. That, as much as anything, captures in microcosm the nature of hitting in MLB today.

A countdown clock toward strike three begins ticking almost the moment a batter takes his place in the box. The league's adjusted OPS+ on the first pitch was higher in 2018 than ever before, and that has been true in most of the last 10 seasons. Batters hit .264/.289/.442 in all plate appearances in which they swung at the first pitch last season, and .241/.330/.395 in all plate appearances in which they took that first offering.

The percentage differences in batting average and isolated power there favor swinging at the first pitch by more than in any season since 1988, while the difference in on-base percentage favors taking by more than ever. If you want to get on base at a decent clip, it's a good idea to be patient, but you run the risk of missing the only chances you'll get to produce power.

New York Yankees 2019

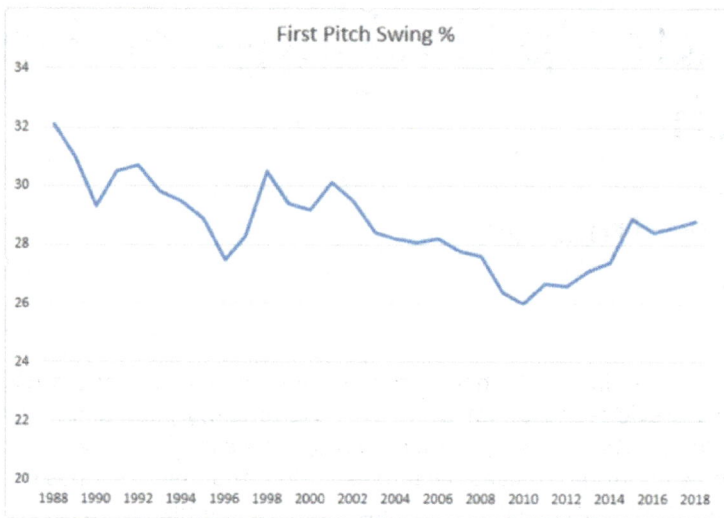

The league swung at the first pitch 28.8 percent of the time in 2018. With the isolated exception of 2015, that's the highest that number has climbed since 2002, but it might not be high enough. With the help of BP research maven Rob McQuown, I looked at the aggregate Called Strike Probability (CSProb) on the first pitch for each season since 2008, when the implementation of PITCHf/x first made measuring that possible. It's risen sharply during that period.

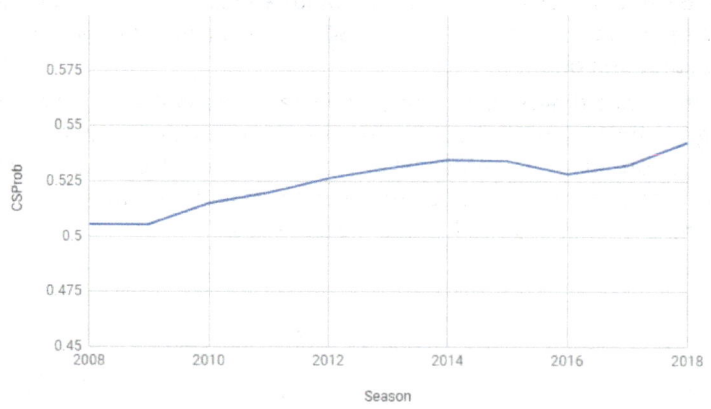

Called Strike Probability, First Pitch of PA (2008-2018)

Called Strike Probability is exactly what it sounds like: a pitch with a given CSProb has roughly that chance of being called a strike, if not swung at. In 2018, a batter who took 100 first pitches from a random sampling of the league's pitchers might expect to fall behind 54 or 55 times—up from 50 or 51 times in 2008. Almost regardless of pitch type (and, notably, especially in the case of fastballs), the first pitch tends to have more of the zone right now than ever before.

Pitchers are better at throwing strikes. They have better stuff, and believe more in their ability to miss bats within the zone. Perhaps most importantly, they know that batters are looking for one thing on the first pitch: a fastball. If they don't get it, they're likely to take the pitch. Check out how the use of sinkers and four-seamers on the first pitch has changed in a decade:

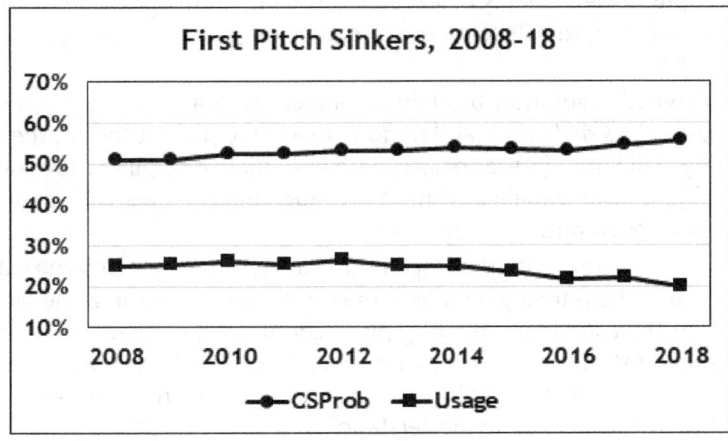

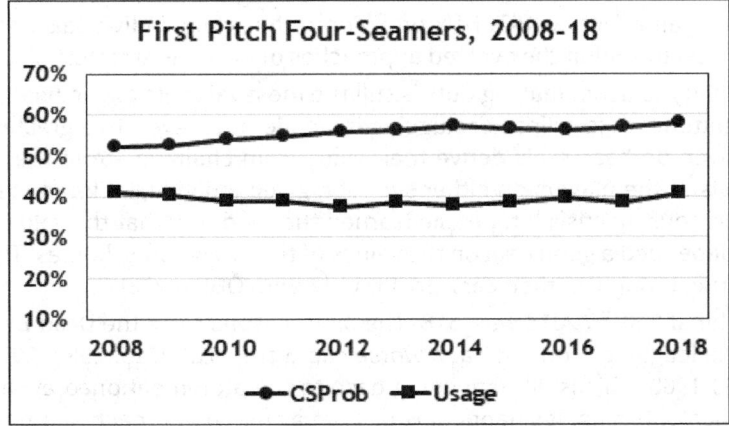

The sinker is losing its place in baseball, but the rate at which pitchers have thrown it on the first pitch hasn't dropped any faster than its usage rate in other counts. Pitchers have actually gone to their four-seamer *more* often to open counts, in the last few years, after a dip in the 2012-2015 period. What's really changed, though, and what shows up in both charts above, is that pitchers are catching more of the zone with first-pitch fastballs than they were a decade ago, or a half-decade ago. They're attacking right away, even with the pitch they know batters are expecting. The message is pretty clear: batters are being too passive.

Sliders, curves, and changeups each have more of the zone when thrown on the first pitch than they did several years ago, too, though the effect is less pronounced. Pitchers have seen the numbers; they know batters are doing better on the first pitch itself. They still feel safe throwing more and better strikes than ever before, figuring they'll come out ahead as long as they keep getting ahead to open each battle.

The Moneyball revolution brought an increased league-wide focus on OBP, which resulted in a de facto mandate to take a more patient tack at the plate. It worked very well for a while, as batters with poor plate discipline were compelled to either adjust or be expelled from the league, and pitchers with poor control were slowly weeded out.

However, concurrent with that revolution, and spurred by it in some ways, was the evolution of the pitching paradigm that now dominates the game. As batters ratcheted up their focus on inflating pitch counts and working walks, pitchers honed theirs on throwing strikes and missing bats. The league's understanding of what makes a good pitcher improved at least as much, from the mid-1990s through the mid-2000s, as its understanding of what makes a good hitter. As amphetamines and other performance-enhancing drugs were phased mostly out of the game, and as PITCHf/x broke onto the scene, individuals and teams learned how to exploit the evolved approaches of even the smartest hitters.

The ability to avoid making outs is still the most valuable one in baseball, but the magnitude of its eclipse of slugging is smaller than ever. To a greater extent than power, on-base skills derive their value from chaining—from the on-base skill levels of the players on either side of a given individual. Eleven years ago, when the housing crisis hit, people learned the hard way that the value of their homes depended a good deal on the values of their neighbors' homes. The same wasn't true, though, of their cars. So it is now, with OBP and SLG.

The global OBP in 2018 was .318. The only seasons since the Dead Ball Era in which the league got on base at a worse clip were 2013-2015, 1988, 1971-1972, and 1963-1968. This is all happening despite the aforementioned evolution of the science of hitting. It's happening despite a shift in approach and focus, one that would steer OBP ever higher, if only it were working.

Instead, it's sitting at a low ebb, and while it does so, even guys who get on base often are a little less helpful than they were 10 years ago—or 20, or 40, or 60, or 70, or 80, or 90. They're less helpful, that is, because unless there happen to be three or four other guys in the lineup who get on just as regularly, their contribution is merely to forestall the inevitable. Runs happen, increasingly, when a sudden bang happens, and that means attacking early in the count—because pitchers are sure as hell doing that.

In a league making contact on barely 75 percent of its swings, and a league in which an increasing number of pitchers can throw multiple off-speed pitches for strikes in any count, the only way to consistently generate offense is going to be aggressive. This isn't necessarily true for individuals, like Mookie Betts and Jose Ramirez, who make a lot of contact and have excellent plate discipline, and whose power comes from such natural quickness in a short stroke. Most players have to make tradeoffs, though, whether it be lowering their contact rate or raising their chase rate, in order to consistently make the quality of contact necessary to survive in today's game.

Highest %	Lowest %
Javier Baez – 48.3	Joe Mauer – 4.6
Freddie Freeman – 47.1	Mookie Betts – 9.7
Ozzie Albies – 46.3	Brett Gardner – 10.7
Jose Altuve – 44.2	Jose Ramirez – 12.0
Nick Castellanos – 44.1	Jason Kipnis – 13.8
Joey Gallo – 42.3	Jesus Aguilar – 14.5
Corey Dickerson – 40.9	Xander Bogaerts – 15.8
Salvador Perez – 40.8	Brian Dozier – 16.3
Eddie Rosario – 40.7	Mike Trout – 17.6
Nick Ahmed – 40.4	Yasmani Grandal – 17.6

Top 10 and Bottom 10 Hitters, First-Pitch Swing Rate (2018)

The question isn't which of these lists one prefers, but what they each convey, qualitatively, about the cat-and-mouse game of early-count hitting. Those top five on the left, especially, drive home the fact that for most players, getting aggressive early in the count is now key to keeping strikeout rate down and hitting for power.

For now, the message is: pitchers are coming right after batters with the nastiest stuff they've ever had. Batters had better stop giving away strike one and force hurlers to adjust, or the global OBP crisis is only going to get worse.

—*Matthew Trueblood is an author of Baseball Prospectus.*

A Hymn for the Index Stat

Patrick Dubuque

We survived without computers. I know this, because I remember the day when my dad hooked up his brand-new Atari 400 computer to the back of our 12-inch Magnavox television, and the perfect blue of the memo pad lit up for the first time. I was born just on the edge of that transitional generation, of learning cursive and balancing checkbooks and just doing math all the time, constant manual arithmetic.

It still amazes me. We learned how to sail ships without computers. We learned how to do calculus. We built towers that didn't fall down, most of the time. We engineered catapults to knock them down anyway. We built a robust system of philosophy called "utilitarianism," founded on the principle that the good of an action is evaluated by summing the effects of that action, which is the kind of formula that would make the world's mainframes crash. The whole foundation of statistics as a field is "here's math you could easily do but would die of old age first."

The fact of the matter is that there is too much math in the world to do. There are too many things changing, and too many things too small to notice, for us to handle. At some point, they become too much for the computers to handle as well, which is why we have chaos theory and undetectable earthquakes, but it's not an even fight. At some point, we fall back on intuition, and given how under-equipped we are, we're forced to bestow that intuition with some sort of supernatural superiority, the "gut feeling," that we can't prove because we can only intuit that our intuition is better.

We're all lousy at intuition, and wonderful at lying to ourselves about it. The honest truth is that computers are far better at intuition than we are, because in order to know what feels "off" you have to know what's "on." In order to do that you have to constantly reassess the average of everything, then re-rank your own experience against it.

Test your own, by comparing these three anonymous lines:

Player	G	HR	AVG	OBP	SLG
Player A	156	38	.259	.342	.535
Player B	154	38	.280	.348	.527
Player C	158	38	.266	.343	.509

These all seem like pretty similar players, right? The second one a touch more batted-ball dependent, the third a little less strong, but all pretty good hitters. And you'd be right, about the latter. Not the former.

Here's the breakdown:

- Player A: 1991 Howard Johnson, 141 DRC+
- Player B: 1996 Dean Palmer, 121 DRC+
- Player C: 2018 Giancarlo Stanton, 114 DRC+

Baseball is fortunate to have escaped the seismic shifts of so many other sports, where the talents and performances of other eras are nearly unrecognizable. (And not just other sports: try to explain the greatness of the movie Duck Soup without adjusting for era.) But they're still there, and they're nearly impossible to account for manually, without having to resort to sweeping generalizations like "steroid era" or juiced-ball era" to throw out entire swathes of production.

This is all to say that we should celebrate the index stat, that simple 100-based scale with such a humble aim: just to give context. It's hard to imagine how we lived without them for so long. Sabermetricians have always tried to make their stats look like other stats: True Average mapped to batting average, FIP molded to look like and compare to ERA. It's easy to understand the motivation—these statistics carry an emotional value in them that is hard to resist, as with the .300 hitter and the 2.00 ERA—but even they fall prey to the same loss of scale as their unadjusted counterparts. If a .300 average means different things in different years, does that hold true for a .300 True Average?

Instead, 100 doesn't say anything, except above average or below. And it does it instantly, for every season in every run environment for any statistic we want it to. We should have more index stats: K%+, so we can stop comparing Mike Clevinger's career 9.46 K/9 to Nolan Ryan's 9.55. HBP%+, so we can note that Ron Hunt was getting plunked when nobody else was getting plunked, as opposed to that imitator Brandon Guyer. Some might note how stale these references are and accuse league-adjustment as a backward-looking drive, and this is true. But we're always looking backward, always comparing the new with the expectations already set. The index stat just forces us to be honest.

There's always resistance to a new statistic, especially one so outwardly simple and so internally complex. We tend to stick with what we know, even in the case of formulas that are supposed to tell us what we know. But if your resistance is that it seems too complicated, too counterintuitive, too "black boxy," I encourage you to consider why you feel that way. Because the real world is infinitely more complicated than baseball, where all the pitches go in one basic direction and the baserunners are only allowed to travel in four directions. Baseball statistics based on mixed methodology are almost impossibly intricate. So are skyscrapers and automobiles. That's why we have computers—to take the guesswork out of them.

—Patrick Dubuque is an author of Baseball Prospectus.

Index of Names

Abreu, Albert 91, 102
Acevedo, Domingo 84, 104
Adams, Chance 47, 101
Andujar, Miguel 18
Betances, Dellin 49
Bird, Greg 20
Breaux, Josh 89, 103
Britton, Zack 51
Cabello, Antonio 89, 96
Cabrera, Oswaldo 89
Cessa, Luis 53
Chapman, Aroldis 55
Contreras, Roansy 85, 99
Coulombe, Daniel 91
Diehl, Phillip 91
Ellsbury, Jacoby 79
Estrada, Thairo 89, 104
Farquhar, Danny 86
Feyereisen, J.P. 91
Florial, Estevan 80, 96
Frazier, Clint 22
Garcia, Deivi 91, 97
Garcia, Dermis 89
Gardner, Brett 24
German, Domingo 57
German, Frank 102
Gil, Luis 87, 98
Gilliam, Isiah 89
Green, Chad 59
Green, Ryder 89
Gregorius, Didi 26

Happ, J.A. 61
Hicks, Aaron 28
Higashioka, Kyle 30
Holder, Jonathan 63
Judge, Aaron 32
Kahnle, Tommy 65
King, Mike 99
Lavarnway, Ryan 89
LeMahieu, DJ 34
Loaisiga, Jonathan 67, 95
Martinez, Nolan 91
Medina, Luis 91, 102
Montgomery, Jordan 88
Nelson, Nick 91
Ottavino, Adam 69
Paxton, James 71
Pereira, Everson 89, 98
Perez, Freicer 91
Romine, Austin 36
Sabathia, CC 73
Sanchez, Gary 38
Sauer, Matt 91
Schmidt, Clarke 91, 100
Seigler, Anthony 81, 101
Severino, Luis 75
Stanton, Giancarlo 41
Stephan, Trevor 91, 104
Stowers, Josh 103
Tanaka, Masahiro 77
Tarpley, Stephen 91
Then, Juan 91

New York Yankees 2019

Torres, Gleyber 43
Tulowitzki, Troy 82
Urshela, Giovanny 89
Voit, Luke 45
Wade, Tyler 83
Whitlock, Garrett 91

Ballpark diagrams for Baseball Prospectus are created by THIRTY81Project, a design concept offering original ballpark artwork, including the new 'Ballparks of 2019' 11 x 17 color print.

Visit **www.thirty81project.com** for full details.